MORE THAN
A CHAIN

Duncan Bhaskaran Brown

The Civic Coach

2018

Praise for more than a chain

More Than a Chain is a must for all those who are taking up a civic role. Not only does it help educate and inform but, with the exercises, it makes you fully understand the expectations, responsibilities & personal skills required. This should be the handbook for civic leaders, their partners and all officers.

Dr Carl Austin-Behan, Lord Mayor of Manchester 2016 – 2017

This book is essential reading for anyone aspiring to be a great civic leader. It's a relevant, straightforward and practical guide to making your mark.

Paul Millward, Chair of the National Association of Civic Officers

Before my election as the 97th Mayor of Worthing, I was very nervous about speaking in public. I would encourage anyone preparing for civic office to read Duncan's book which can help you be fully prepared. I wish I had read this before I became mayor. It is the best book on civic leadership this century.

Bob Smytherman #CoolMayor of Worthing

This is an incredible guide for someone coming into office. Every single aspect of being a civic leader is highlighted here. It is a wonderful handbook of who to meet, how to choose your charities, what you can achieve, in short everything it takes to be a great civic leader.

Mimi Harker OBE, Chairman Chiltern District Council 2015 - 2017

A useful tool for every incoming Mayor. This is a must for anyone who wishes to have a successful civic year in the world as it is now. I wouldn't hesitate to put it into the hands of any Deputy Mayor; it is an induction programme all in one book.

Tracy Frisby, Civic Services Team Manager North East Lincolnshire Council

The world is changing, you can't just engage people face to face any more. You need to meet people online too. Duncan has really got to grips with this vital part of community engagement.

Anne-Marie Lategan, Social Media Start Up

More than a Chain is a must-read for aspiring and sitting mayors. The ultimate guide for life just before, during and post your mayoral term. I wish this book had been published before I took office as Mayor of Croydon.

Wayne Trakas-Lawlor, Mayor of Croydon 2016 - 2017

No one really tells you what you're supposed to do when you become mayor, but Duncan has broken down preparing for office into a series of manageable steps. I recommend this to anyone even thinking of becoming a civic leader.

Samantha Bowring, Leader Abingdon-on-Thames Town Council

Duncan is a breath of fresh air. He is part of the new breed of civic dignitaries who want to retain old traditions and also move with the times. The down to earth, relevant and entertaining way that he imparts his advice would have been so useful. Every new civic leader should read this book.

Lynne Sparks, Mayor of Welwyn Hatfield 2017 - 2018

©2018 Duncan Bhaskaran Brown

First published in Great Britain in 2018 by The Civic Coach

www.theciviccoach.com

The moral right of the author has been asserted

A catalogue record for this book is available from the British Library

Book and cover design by Andrew Conway-Hyde

ISBN: 978-1-9999665-1-5

First Edition: March 2018

10 9 8 7 6 5 4 3 2 1

For Sreeja

More than a Mayoress

23/10/21

To Sue

Enjoy

Contents

THE RISE OF THE TWENTY-FIRST CENTURY MAYORS

"The public perception of a mayor was an old Victorian gentleman. I wanted to break down some misconceptions".

Glen Chisholm, Mayor of Ipswich 2015-2016

On 1st April 1974, the Local Government Act changed the role of mayors forever. They no longer led their councils. They no longer acted as chief magistrate. It seemed they had lost all their power. It seemed they had lost their ability to have an impact on their communities

But they didn't seem to mind. For years mayors and council chairs led a jolly little existence. The most onerous thing they had to do was to stay sober long enough to greet passing royals. Mostly they could swan around with their big gold chain in their tax-funded limos. They got on very nicely, thank you very much.

Then things changed. The world moved on, people moved on, councils moved on. But civic dignitaries didn't. They didn't move with the times. They failed to spot that no one was impressed by a politician pretending to be an aristocrat. They failed to notice that council budgets got torn to shreds. They failed to realise that people wanted more than a chain.

Sadly there are a lot of mayors and council chairs who are still like that. You will find them anywhere that the catering is good and there is an opportunity for splendour and ceremony. I call them buffet munchers. And you can be just like them: you too can be just a chain.

It is very easy. All you need to do is put yourself first. Don't worry about your council or your community and only do things that benefit you. Make sure that everyone you meet massages your ego and makes you feel important. Take every opportunity for spectacle and self-aggrandizement. Surround yourself with people who pander to your ambition and snobbery.

Most important of all, *munch that buffet*. If that sounds attractive then put this book back in the envelope, send it to me and I'll refund your money, because this book is not for you.

No thanks

You are not like that. You bought this book because you want to make the most of this chance. You bought this book because you are worried about living up to the responsibility of the office. But most of all you bought this book because you want to make a difference to your community.

This is great, because being a civic leader gives you fantastic opportunities. It gives you the chance to provide a human face for your council. It gives you the chance to take your council's message to new sections of the community. It gives you the unique opportunity to connect your council to your community.

If that sounds better than chowing down on a few buffets and making yourself feel important then read on. You are among friends.

Meet Carol

Carol was honoured when she found her name was going forward to become mayor of her home town. She was excited about the opportunity but very nervous about doing a good job. She asked around her council and people gave her advice yet none of it allayed her fears. As she took office she had a nagging doubt that she just wasn't ready.

During her time in office she met many great people and her confidence grew. The more she gave speeches the better she found it. The more she was interviewed the easier it became. As the year drew on her skills blossomed. She was transformed.

But something more important happened. She began to realise the full potential of the office she held. She began to understand its reach, its influence, its power. She began to see how she could use it as a platform to make a long term difference to her community.

Finally she was ready. She had the skills, she had the confidence, and she had a plan. And that was when she stepped down.

All too common

It happens again and again. It is a pity that so many people only find the confidence in their own abilities as they are leaving office. It is a shame that so many people only develop the skills they need while in office rather than hitting the ground running.

But worst of all so many people only realise the opportunity they have as it disappears. That is surely the easiest way to make sure you spend the rest of your life regretting what might have been. Do you want to look back on this special year knowing that you could have done more?

I don't want that to happen to you. I don't want you to finish your time in office and look back with disappointment. I don't want you to feel like you could have achieved more. I don't want you to be filled with regret.

To make sure this does not happen you are going to need to prepare properly. That will involve honing your skills, developing a clear plan and getting some support. But it will also require you understanding what the office can achieve. That is not something you are going to get from a typical self-centred old school mayor.

Introducing the twenty-first century mayor

When Alex Maskey became the first Sinn Fein Lord Mayor of Belfast he did something unprecedented. He laid a wreath at the cenotaph to commemorate the battle of the Somme, an act unthinkable to many nationalists. This gesture was the start of a year of reconciliation, marked by a real commitment to ending sectarian violence. Alex Maskey did a huge amount to bring together one of the most divided communities in the United Kingdom. He had a huge impact.

The good news is there are lots more twenty-first century mayors like Alex Maskey. The good news is that you *do not* have to be a buffet muncher you can be a mayor for your time. You can be a twenty-first century mayor.

A job description for a twenty-first century civic leader

It might seem strange to have to give you a job description but, all the standing orders and all the mayoral handbooks, fail to provide an adequate description of what a twenty-first century mayor does. They use words like ceremonial, honorary and traditional. These words say the position isn't important, isn't relevant and certainly isn't at the centre of what the council does.

Instead, here are some examples of what great civic leaders have done. How they have served their council. How they have had an impact on their community.

 Twenty-first century mayor

Lynne Sparks had seen too many photos where the mayor wasn't even smiling. When she became mayor of Welwyn Hatfield she was determined to change that. Friendly, outgoing and down to earth, she is a twenty-first century mayor showing people that they have a twenty-first century council.

The face of the council

To a sizable proportion of the community the mayor or council chair *is* the council. You may be the only person from the council that they meet. The reputation of the council sits on your shoulders.

You must ask yourself a question: how do you want people to think of your council? Do you want them to think of it as stuffy, pompous and out-of-date? Or do you want them to think of it as warm, friendly and relevant? If you follow Lynne's example you can use your role to change people's perception of your council.

The council spokesperson

To a sizable proportion of the community the mayor is the voice of the council. The chance to spread your council's message to every section of the community is yours.

Twenty-first century mayor

When Darryn Causby became Lord Mayor he was elected by an entirely new council. He realised the merger of Armagh, Bainbridge and Craigavon councils was a cause for concern for residents. He allayed their fears by sharing the council's new vision at hundreds of events in his community.

Without doubt your council will have many things they would like their community to know. You are about to be given privileged access to every section of your community. Do you want to use the opportunity to tell people how important you are? You, like Darryn, can help people understand what their council is doing for them.

 Twenty-first century mayor

Bob Smythersman gets social media. He uses it to help people connect with each other. When he became Mayor of Worthing it was an obvious way for him to connect his community with his council. But he went further than social media and built connections throughout his community.

The connection with the community

Being the face and spokesperson of the council means it is your job to connect your council to your community. But a bridge works both ways. A great civic leader takes what they have learnt about the area and brings it into the council. They share the knowledge and experience they have gained with other councillors and staff to help them better understand, and ultimately serve, their community.

If you follow Bob's lead you have the chance to bring your council and your citizens closer.

Your journey

That should have got you thinking about the important role good civic leaders play and the many things you could achieve while in office. You might even be wondering how you are going to go from where you are today to being a fully-fledged civic leader. That transformation has five sections.

Understanding

You will need to understand your council and the role that you are going to undertake, but most of all you will need to understand yourself. You will take an in-depth look at what you are passionate about and what you are good at.

Vision

You are going to develop a vision. It will come from your skills, your passion and your opportunities. It will be one you can implement and it will be a vision that makes the most of your situation.

Recruitment

You will often be alone; you will often have to rely on yourself. But being a civic leader is a team game. Ultimately you will achieve much more if you have people by your side. You will look at what sort of support you will need and how best to pick your line-up.

Alignment

You won't achieve much if your council stands in your way. You cannot get everyone to agree with everything but if you can understand their doubts you will find a way to progress. If everyone from the council is clear about what you are trying to achieve you will have a much more successful year.

Planning

This is where you will pull everything together. That might sound like the hard part but much of the work will have been done in the other sections so actually planning will be the easy bit. Once that is done you will be the end of this journey.

Of course the end of this book is just the beginning of the adventure. The real journey will begin once you take office.

That is the plan

Don't rush through this book. Each chapter takes about half an hour to read but that is the easy bit. The exercises in each chapter will take you another hour or two. This can be challenging. You have many other demands on your time but you are also good at juggling.

The real question is: how much time do you have before you take office? Obviously if you have got a month then you will have to get through it all in a month. If you have three months, take longer. You should work out how many weeks you have before you take office. Do the maths below, you can get a calculator if you can't remember your thirteen times table.

Number of weeks till you take office: ....

Divide by thirteen chapters: ....

Number of chapters you should read per week: ....

You might want to keep your notes together

There is a workbook to help you containing all the exercises in this book in PDF form. If you print it out you will have more space to let your ideas run wild and even doodle a bit. You can download it for free here: *www.theciviccoach.com/mtc-workbook/*.

It is called a workbook because it does involve work. You are going to need to do many things which will stretch you. You are going to need to do many things that will be difficult. You may even have to do things that will make you question whether this is the right path for you.

But after all of that you will be prepared. You will be set to take office and that work *will* pay dividends. You will be ready. Once you have completed this book you will have:

- The skills you need to be a great civic leader

- A clear vision for you time in office

- A magnificent team to help you implement it

- The support of your council leaders and staff

- A brilliant one page civic business plan

All of that adds up to you offering real value to your council and leaving a lasting impression on your community. What could be more satisfying than that?

Get going

To live up to the potential of the office, to live up to your potential, there is a lot for you to do. You *can* provide a human face for your council. You can share its important messages across the community. You *can* be a genuine connection between local government and the people. You *can* be more than a chain.

There is no longer a place for civic dignitaries because your community doesn't need dignitaries. Your community needs leaders. The time of the buffet munchers is over. It is time for the twenty-first century mayors.

UNDERSTANDING

BEGIN WITH YOU

I've really enjoyed being mayor "my way".

Lynne Sparks, Mayor of Welwyn Hatfield 2017-2018

How do you feel?

You are excited. Of course you are, it is a massive honour to get this job. You will meet some amazing people, go to some amazing places and develop in amazing ways. This is the start of something special.

You are afraid. Of course you are, there is a massive responsibility that goes with this job. You will have to do things that are challenging, things that are hard and things that are well outside your comfort zone.

That is what being a civic leader is about, excitement tinged with fear. Don't worry everyone is like that. The trick is to concentrate on the excitement and where it will take you. Keep in mind everything you are going to achieve and the huge, lasting impact you will have on your community.

You are going to begin your journey by looking at yourself. It is important to start with you because you need to build from the foundations up. You must be the basis of this whole experience. So you need to get thinking about every aspect of yourself. While this is an important part of the process, it can get you thinking about issues you don't want to. It can force you to consider things you don't do so well. You may even have to confront your flaws. Looking in the mirror can be tough.

But at the heart of this process is developing a vision for your time in office. The important thing is that it is *your* vision. And it can't be your vision without you. By understanding your skills and your passions you can discover what you can do. But more than that you will begin to discover what you *must* do. That will develop a truly special vision. And that should get you excited.

Begin with you
What will success feel like?

- Start by thinking about how your accomplishments will feel.

What kind of civic leader are you going to be?

- There are many ways to approach the office, what will yours be?

How will it affect your health?

- It is important to keep an eye on your wellbeing.

What skills do you have?

- You need to work out where your strengths lie.

Where will you get the skills you need?

- You aren't good at everything so how are you going to cross these bridges?

What will success feel like?

Start with the day you leave office

What will it feel like to leave office? That might seem like an odd place to start. While being a civic leader is one of the most rewarding jobs in local politics it is also hard work. You have a lot to do because preparing properly is also hard work. While it is well worth the effort it may not always seem that way so you need motivation to fall back on.

Motivation is the fuel that fires our actions. It can come from many places but it is not always readily available. By dreaming about the successful outcome of your time in office you will fire yourself up for the work ahead. By recalling it you can find your way through the tough times.

Ready your imagination

You will get the most out of this exercise if you let go and see where your dreams take you. It is not about what you are going to do. It is about feeling not thinking. It is not about planning, it is about dreaming. Go wild.

You are going to describe the feeling as you finish your time in office. There is no limit to what you write down; you aren't trying to produce some masterful prose. What you are after is the emotion and the experience – the congratulations, the applause, the respect, the pride and the sense of a job well done. Try to capture anything that will make you feel great about your time in office.

You could write about something specific like "Joe congratulates me on organising an excellent community event," but the details are not important. What they are congratulating you for is not important. Think about how these congratulations will make you feel.

The day you leave office

....

....

....

....

....

You are going to feel great when you have finished. That is because you are going to do a great job and the reason you will is because you have committed to doing it the right way. Keep these positive feeling in mind whenever it seems to be getting hard. Remember that you are working toward those wonderful feelings.

What kind of civic leader are you going to be?

The process of self-discovery benefits from concentration. It seems unlikely that you have cleared your desk and set about reading this with zero distractions. Maybe you are on the bus, maybe you are eating lunch. These occasions are not necessarily the best time for deep thinking; it may be better to have a look through the questions and make some notes. Then return to them when you have more time.

This exercise is designed to get you thinking about what you are going to do while in office. You are going to look at what interests you, what you care about and what lights your fire. Later you will develop these ideas into a vision for your year but for the moment ignore any preconceptions you may have.

WHAT KIND OF CIVIC LEADER ARE YOU GOING TO BE?	
What kind of work do you find most rewarding?	
What do you care about deeply?	
Who do you admire and why?	
What makes you most satisfied?	
How do you personally want to change while in office?	
When you look back on your year what do you want people to say?	
What is the one thing you want to achieve while in office?	
What do you want to be remembered for?	

Get the workbook

All the exercises in this book are in a downloadable workbook. You can get this for free at *www.theciviccoach.com/mtc-workbook/* The workbook isn't just a great way to keep all your notes together but it also has more space for your answers.

How will it affect your health?

You cannot imagine the range of opportunities you will get as a civic leader. You will be given privileged access to some amazing places. Which is great. But it is also demanding. You will need a lot of energy as you will be living life at a fast pace. This means you will have to look after yourself.

The problem is that the civic lifestyle does not tend to be healthy. You will be offered a lot of alcohol and unhealthy food. You will often be short of time so it will be hard to exercise or sleep properly. While you are out and about having these amazing experiences you may well find it hard to keep on top of your wellbeing. To prepare you for this you are going to take a moment to rate your current levels of health

This is not a scientific test but it should quickly point out if you have an area of concern. This book is not about health and fitness so it will not provide you with the answers to any wellbeing questions you have. All I can do is warn you that amazing as the civic merry go round is it does have challenges for your wellness.

YOUR DIET IS:

Poor   Very good

1   10

YOU EXERCISE:

Never   Regularly

1   10

YOU DRINK:

Too much   Nothing

1   10

If you've any concerns about these areas then you need to think about how you're going to cope with the demands of the office. Spend some time making a plan. A year is a long time. If you are really worried consult your GP.

What skills do you have?

A unique set of skills

You *do not* have all the skills you need to become a civic leader. You are in good company – no one does. That is because it demands a very specific yet wide-ranging set of abilities. While in office you will use all these:

Communication Skills

- Interpersonal skills

- Public speaking

- Chairing meetings

- Using the media

- Engaging online

- Hosting events

Leadership Skills

- Organisation

- Developing a vision

- Recruitment

- Persuasion

- Management

- Planning

This skills audit is one of the most rewarding exercises you will do. It has the potential to shape how you approach the office, that is very exciting. Yet it is a challenging exercise. It involves really looking at yourself and it takes time to complete. But the rewards are worth the effort. The clarity that you will achieve will have an impact on your time in office.

You've heard the expression play to your strengths and that's not a bad strategy. This is an exercise to show you what you are good at and what areas you can shine in. It's not meant to point out what you can't do. It's not about showing how much you should learn.

How the audit works

If you have a lot of experience or a well-developed skill you will give yourself 5; if you have no experience you will score 1. Average them out to find your overall score for each section.

Make sure you're in the right frame of mind before you tackle this. The best thing to do is to look through the questions now and jot down some initial answers. You can then revisit them and complete it properly in the workbook.

SKILLS DEVELOPMENT PLAN

SKILL:	CURRENT LEVEL:	DESIRED LEVEL:
TRAINING		**PRACTICE**

SKILL:	CURRENT LEVEL:	DESIRED LEVEL:
TRAINING		**PRACTICE**

SKILL:	CURRENT LEVEL:	DESIRED LEVEL:
TRAINING		**PRACTICE**

PUBLIC SPEAKING

How comfortable are you with speaking to large groups of people?

UNCOMFORTABLE	1	2	3	4	5	COMFORTABLE

How much experience do you have in speaking outside your council?

NONE	1	2	3	4	5	LOTS

How often have you spoken on a wide range of subjects?

NEVER	1	2	3	4	5	OFTEN

How comfortable are you speaking to children or young adults?

UNCOMFORTABLE	1	2	3	4	5	COMFORTABLE

How much experience do you have at impromptu speaking?

NONE	1	2	3	4	5	LOTS

TOTAL SCORE		AVERAGE SCORE	

CHAIRING

How much experience do you have at chairing committees?

NONE	1	2	3	4	5	LOTS

How many meetings have you chaired outside of your council?

NONE	1	2	3	4	5	LOTS

How comfortable are you following the agenda when it gets difficult?

UNCOMFORTABLE	1	2	3	4	5	COMFORTABLE

How familiar are you with your council's standing orders?

UNFAMILIAR	1	2	3	4	5	FAMILIAR

How good are you at thinking on your feet?

POOR	1	2	3	4	5	GREAT

TOTAL SCORE		AVERAGE SCORE	

YOUR HABITS

YOUR DIET IS:

Poor   Very good

1 — 10

YOU EXERCISE:

Never   Regularly

1 — 10

YOU DRINK:

Too much   Nothing

1 — 10

YOUR SLEEP IS:

Poor   Very good

1 — 10

YOU HANDLE STRESS:

Badly   Very well

1 — 10

YEAR PLANNER

MARCH	APRIL	MAY

JUNE	JULY	AUGUST

SEPTEMBER	OCTOBER	NOVEMBER

DECEMBER	JANUARY	FEBRUARY

MARCH	APRIL	MAY

YEAR PLANNER

MAY	JUNE	JULY

AUGUST	SEPTEMBER	OCTOBER

NOVEMBER	DECEMBER	JANUARY

FEBRUARY	MARCH	APRIL

MANAGEMENT

How good are you at asking people to do things for you?						
POOR	1	2	3	4	5	GREAT

How much do you enjoy matching people's skills to tasks?						
NOT AT ALL	1	2	3	4	5	A LOT

How comfortable are you with delegating?						
UNCOMFORTABLE	1	2	3	4	5	COMFORTABLE

How often do you give feedback?						
NEVER	1	2	3	4	5	OFTEN

How good are you at helping different people get on?						
POOR	1	2	3	4	5	GREAT

TOTAL SCORE		AVERAGE SCORE	

PLANNING

How often have you turned a vision into a series of goals?						
NEVER	1	2	3	4	5	OFTEN

How good are you at turning a goal into a series of actions?						
POOR	1	2	3	4	5	GREAT

How much experience do you have in organising large events?						
NONE	1	2	3	4	5	A LOT

How much experience do you have in developing long-term plans?						
NONE	1	2	3	4	5	A LOT

How comfortable are you with collating information?						
UNCOMFORTABLE	1	2	3	4	5	COMFORTABLE

TOTAL SCORE		AVERAGE SCORE	

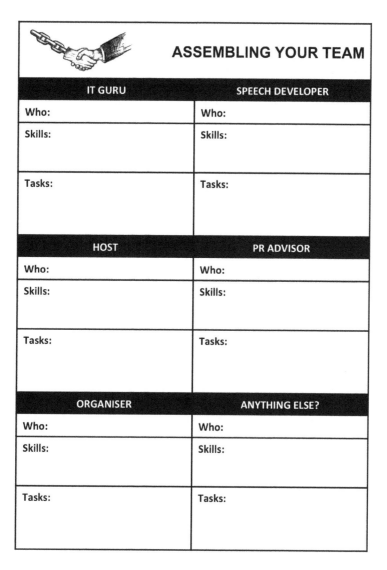

ASSEMBLING YOUR TEAM	
IT GURU	**SPEECH DEVELOPER**
Who:	Who:
Skills:	Skills:
Tasks:	Tasks:
HOST	**PR ADVISOR**
Who:	Who:
Skills:	Skills:
Tasks:	Tasks:
ORGANISER	**ANYTHING ELSE?**
Who:	Who:
Skills:	Skills:
Tasks:	Tasks:

Once you have completed all the questions and averages take a quick look back through them. The first time people do this exercise they tend to rate themselves close to the middle of the spectrum.

If all your scores have come out looking a little bit too similar it is worth going through them again. As you are not in the middle for everything then this isn't an accurate reflection of where you are. Your results should be a mixture of highs, middles and lows. Once you are happy that your scores really represent you it is time to plot them on the chart.

These charts should give you a clear view of where you might improve and what you do well. Then the following chapters will cover these skills. They should help you to think about how you can improve. But before you think about that you should consider whether you will use all these skills or not.

Where will you get the skills you need?

Many tasks need many skills

Being a civic leader is about using what you have got. Some skills are not negotiable: you will need them. Other skills are only necessary if you are going to concentrate on certain areas.

Which are the most important skills?

Before you start to worry that you have a skills shortage you need to consider the two types of skill.

- Must-have skills

- Programme-dependant skills

Must-have skills

You absolutely cannot get by without solid interpersonal skills. This is non-negotiable. It comes into everything you will do. If you have any concerns about your people-skills make developing them a priority.

You will be asked to speak in public. You will also need leadership skills, especially organisation. You are going to become a leader, all your leadership skills will be called on at some point.

Programme-dependent skills

You will have to chair meetings. You will be interviewed by the media. These are things that you will do – so why aren't they must-have skills? It is because you won't be using them that often. You will chair full council meetings at most ten times. If you don't do it well you won't be popular with other councillors but the public won't care. So it depends on what you are doing. If you need lots of support from your fellow councillors then chairing is important. If you don't then maybe it's better to focus your limited time elsewhere.

Again, if you aren't great in the media they won't interview you as much. Will that hurt your overall programme? If your programme requires press promotion then it is a problem. That is the point. You will need some skills more and some less depending on what you are trying to achieve. In essence, you need to develop a vision that you have the skills to implement. You might choose to improve some skills so you can achieve more. Just don't aim at a total skills overhaul.

The skills you haven't got

That said, if you are short in an area that you would like to work in you can always find someone who has those skills. Leadership is about finding the right people and using their skills. Don't be down if you think you are missing a key skill: your team can help.

How do you develop the areas you are weaker in?

The other alternative is to improve your own skills. There are two ways to do this: practise or training.

Practise

If you have a skill but don't feel it is developed enough for the task ahead then you should practise to improve it. Many of the techniques you will need

> ### Quick Win
>
> Do you want to practise your media skills? The next time someone asks you a question try answering like you're being interviewed on TV.

can be practised in your everyday life and there are exercises in the following chapter to help you do that.

Training

If you're particularly weak in an area then training is the way to go. This will teach you the skills that you need. Once you have learnt you can then refine the skill with practise.

Maybe your council offers some training that you can take advantage of. Can your civic team recommend someone or somewhere? There are many great training companies out there and there are more and more opportunities to learn online.

It is possible that you are worried about the cost of training. It can be expensive, but you will receive an allowance from your council. It seems sensible to spend some of that on developing the skills you need to do the job. Investing in yourself is never a waste of money.

Skills development plan

You might be thinking, "I need to work on everything!" Firstly, take a moment to remember that if you have been asked to become a civic leader people clearly recognise that you do have ability. Secondly, unless you have a lot of time that isn't going to be possible to work on everything. You need to work out which skill you are going to prioritise then concentrate on it. You may want to add two other skills that you can also hone. But make sure you don't try to take on too much. Use the form below to help you think about where you should focus.

Once you've written down a few ideas you might need to do some research before you can get started. Whatever you decide, get practicing, get training.

 **ONLINE STRATEGY SHEET**

What are you good at?

What is being done well now?

How much time do you have?	Per day:	Per week:
Who will help?	What will they do?	

What will you achieve?	What medium will you use?

☐ Informing
☐ Outreach
☐ Promoting

☐ Blog
☐ Video

☐ Facebook
☐ Twitter

Where will you post?

☐ Your website
☐ Council's website

☐ Facebook
☐ Twitter

☐ YouTube
☐ Other: _____

What will you post?

How will you tell people what you are doing?

What do you need to do before you take office?

You are complicated

You are a multifaceted person that is why there is a lot to consider. Spend some time thinking back to these exercises over the next week. You may even want to revisit them. But above all remember within you is everything you need. You're good enough. You're already a leader.

What to do now

What will success feel like?

- You have spent some time imagining success. Keep this feeling in mind as you go through the programme. There is a lot to do: the sense of achievement should be your motivation.

Have you completed the exercises?

- Get the workbook at *www.theciviccoach.com/mtc-workbook/* and make sure you have completed all the exercises from this section. Give them the time they deserve.

How will it affect your health?

- Think about how to stay healthy, even consider seeking professional advice.

Do you have the skills you need?

- Complete the skills-development plan. Begin some research into ways to practise or train and start thinking of people you can recruit to make up for areas you aren't skilled in.

Diving into Your Council

"Our time is now and I challenge all members of the council to embrace the exciting challenges that lie ahead".

Wayne Trakas-Lawlor, Mayor of Croydon 2016-2017

Take a deep dive

These are exciting times. You are doing important work. By identifying how you will feel when you have accomplished everything, you have given yourself a boast of motivation. Remember it is always there when you need it. And you will need it, there is still a long way between here and the finish line. The number of things you need to do may feel daunting. It is common to feel overwhelmed. But by continuing your journey of preparation you can have the impact that you felt in that exercise. Within you is everything you need to be a fantastic civic leader. You are only beginning to unlock that potential; there is a lot more to come.

You are going to spend a lot of time refining your vision of what you can achieve while in office. You certainly have some thoughts already but before you run away with them you need to take a look at the job from your council's point of view. If you know what it expects you to do you can set your plans on a firm footing. Of course, finding out what your council expects of you isn't always easy. It will be complicated for you to uncover all the information that you need. At some points you may even think that it has been set up to stop you finding out what you need to. Understanding your council is a tough assignment.

But like so much of what you are doing, it will be worth the effort. Having a clear idea of how you will work with your council means there will be no surprises. This will help because there will be enough other stuff to keep you on your toes. You don't need councillors unexpectedly creating issues at the wrong moment.

Diving into your council

What are the responsibilities of the position?

- There is a lot to do, but what?

What support will you get?

- Hopefully there are a lot of people who are going to be there for you.

What do you have to do?

- There is no job description, what are you supposed to do?

What opportunities are there?

- There are a lot of great prospects, you need to find them.

Why you need to build relationships

- Relationships are at the heart of being more than a chain.

Who you need to meet

- It is time to start talking about what is going to happen.

What are the responsibilities of the position?

While it is important to start by thinking about yourself and what you want to achieve, you also need to remember that you aren't the only person in this relationship. You will have to think about what your council needs and what they're expecting from you.

And you can bet your bottom dollar that they will be thinking about you. The sad truth is that many people think they are uniquely qualified to tell you what to do. Councillors who have fulfilled the office will be quick to tell you that you should do it their way. Members of the public will also weigh in with their idea of what a civic leader should be.

You are going to try to find out what you are expected to do when you're in office. People have opinions, people have beliefs, many of these contradict one another. Which makes it impossible to fulfil all of these expectations but it is still useful to know them.

There are four things you need to be aware of:

- What you are legally obliged to do

- What the standing orders say you should do

- What custom and practice obliges you to do

- What people will expect you to do

First, the only thing that you will be legally obliged to do is to chair full council meetings. That might surprise you but it is the only thing you really must do.

The standing orders are the self-determined set of rules that a council chooses to operate by. In practice it is pretty hard to enforce any job description they may contain. They usually talk about you taking a lead at civic occasions and being an ambassador for your community. These are the things that your council has decided their mayor is to do. They were probably decided years ago and haven't been looked at since. Should the council decide that you shouldn't do them it would be possible to change them.

There is much that custom and practice dictates you should do. It is often nothing more than tradition that compels you to appoint a chaplain and arrange a civic service. Finally there are the things that people think you should do, such as not take holidays, always wear a tie and be an Anglican. They have no basis in law or reality but people still expect you to do them.

Beyond these basics the question remains: what do you have to do?

Tension

There is a tension. On the one hand, there are myriad things that you are expected to do. On the other there is what you want to achieve. Being a successful civic leader is about balancing these often opposing forces.

You can't please all people

Added to the tension of your aims versus other people's expectations are your various responsibilities. You have a responsibility to your council: part of being a civic leader is about serving your council. You have a responsibility to your political party: they provided the means that got you into office. But above all you have a responsibility to your community. After all you got involved in local politics to serve your community.

The aims and objective of these groups won't always line up. How do you resolve these tensions? Do you do what your council expects, even if it is to the detriment of your own aims? Do you pursue your own aims to the detriment of your party? Do you serve the community even if it is to the detriment of your council? These are difficult questions.

You must find your own answers. But there will be tension between what you need to do and what people expect you to do.

What does your council do?

It sounds stupid, but do you know what your council does? It is likely you do. Still, it is important to be very clear on the subject. You are about to become the most visible councillor in your community. If you aren't sure familiarise yourself with your council's services and how it relates to other tiers of local government and other public-sector organisations. You should do this before you do anything else. People will ask you questions about everything from rubbish bins to infrastructure development.

What support will you get?

The civic team

> **Quick Win**
>
> When can you say hello to your civic team? Put it into your diary now. Commit to building or improving those relationships.

Your civic team is about to become the most important part of the council. They vary from one part-time secretary to a full-blown events and engagement team. You need to find out about your civic office. You should already have a good idea of how it is set up but it is important to be crystal clear about how they work. A misunderstanding about responsibilities can sour a relationship; the *last thing* you want to do is annoy your secretary.

Civic team quiz

You could do this from memory but it is better if you pop in and ask some questions. That way you will know what to expect.

CIVIC ONE-SHEET

Your vision in one line:	
Vision Section	
PROJECT 1	
Aim of project	
PROJECT 2	
Aim of project	
PROJECT 3	
Aim of project	
Vision Section	
PROJECT 1	
Aim of project	
PROJECT 2	
Aim of project	
PROJECT 3	
Aim of project	
Vision Section	
PROJECT 1	
Aim of project	
PROJECT 2	
Aim of project	
PROJECT 3	
Aim of project	

I cannot stress this too much: it is very important to make sure you know what your team expects from you and what you can expect from them. If the expectations are clear you will have a happy and productive relationship.

What do you have to do?

The civic package

There is no job description for your role. There are no standard operating procedures to follow. That is because it is almost impossible to fathom everything a civic leader should do. Even when you have finished you still won't know everything that was expected of you.

That said, there might be a handbook. Some councils have them, some don't. Some are comprehensive, some are out of date. Yours might be helpful. There might be an induction programme. These tend to be quite good as they are generally provided by more forward-thinking officers.

However they plan to ease you into the office there will be a problem. Civic handbooks and induction programmes are written by civic officers. This means they represent the concerns of civic officers. They tell you the things that civic officers want you to know. This is useful but only part of the story.

So if you get a handbook grab a copy; if there is a programme take part wholeheartedly and be grateful for the support. It is a start. If you haven't been given anything don't worry. You are going to build our own programme.

Your personalised civic handbook

This is the beginning of your own induction programme. You will be looking at the following:

- Significant events and events that involve a lot of work

- Appointing a chaplain

- The various other offices that you will hold

- What to wear

- A non-political role

These things require a lot of thinking, and a lot of work because there are a lot of expectations. Once you know about them you will know where you stand. This will be invaluable when planning.

The rhythm of the year

Your time in office will have a rhythm. In fact, it will practically have a life of its own. You need to find out what it looks and feels like.

You cannot possibly hope to know everything that will happen so you are going to concentrate on major events. Firstly, events that are significant for what they are: Remembrance Sunday, for example. Secondly, the events that will involve a lot of planning and organisation on your part: charity events and the like.

Hopefully you will have a good idea of what the civic year looks like. Fill out the diagram below. It may take you a few goes to remember everything. If you are struggling don't worry as we'll come back to it. You will take office in May but March and April are on too. There may be important handover meetings then.

YEAR PLANNER

MARCH	APRIL	MAY

JUNE	JULY	AUGUST

SEPTEMBER	OCTOBER	NOVEMBER

DECEMBER	JANUARY	FEBRUARY

MARCH	APRIL	MAY

August

Most people who fill out this exercise notice a big hole in August. Very little happens in high summer. This is excellent. August is the time to recharge your batteries. I strongly suggest that you take a holiday at that time. Take two weeks. Do something that relaxes you – something that really helps you unwind. And do not feel guilty about it.

Of course there are some places that are busy during August – generally because of the tourist industry. If this is the case, find another time during the year that you can take a well-deserved break.

Who will you appoint as your chaplain?

This can be very easy or surprisingly thorny. If you belong to a church, a mosque or a temple it is simple. Of course you want your minister, imam or priest to be your chaplain.

If you have no strong convictions either way it is an easy decision. Appoint the parish priest and let them get on with it. Once that is done you don't have to worry about things like who will do the prayers before council meetings or how the civic service will pan out. You can spend your valuable time worrying about the things that are important to you.

The problem comes when you *aren't* religious and you have strong feeling on the subject. This means you will not be happy simply appointing the local Anglican minister and forgetting about it.

If you would rather not have a religious chaplain, then you may be able to find a local humanist who can fill the office. But be warned that this may not go down to well with your fellow councillors.

Or you may think that religion has no place in politics. You may not want to appoint a chaplain at all. You could try that. If you don't appoint a chaplain then there is the danger of your council doing it for you.

 Twenty-first century mayor

The Mayor of Ipswich has a multi faith event. It is held in a neutral venue and involves members from all the town's faith groups. It is a fantastic community event but more than that the committee that runs it is a great resource for community cohesion.

I have no idea what your fellow councillors will or won't let you do but this can be an emotive issue so be careful. If you want to do anything that's out of the ordinary you should start negotiations now.

If you want to do something that is against the will of most of the council you need to ask yourself if it is something that you care about enough to get involved in a fight. It may well be better to save your energy and use it on an issue that you really care about.

Associated roles

You will have some ex-officio roles. You will probably have titles such as President of this and Governor of that. Some will be prestigious. Some will be strange.

 Twenty-first century mayor

Lord Mayor of Chester is also the Admiral of the River Dee. The honour was bestowed on office-holder in 1354 by Edward the Black Prince. The title used to allow them to collect taxes for the crown. Now it is just a fascinating extra aspect of being Lord Mayor.

Most organisations will have a good idea of what your level of commitment will be. They will be happy if you turn up at the AGM and press the flesh. Technically, some will come with a workload. This is particularly true if you are a trustee of a charity. You may view it as an honouree role but trustees are liable for any financial issue that arise in a charity. If you are signing anything, you should be aware of the responsibility you are taking on.

What is the dress code?

Most events don't have a dress code. This can cause you a problem – you don't want to look either overdressed or underdressed. You will tend to just dress smart but sometimes it looks a bit over-formal when most of the audience is running around in shorts, t-shirts and flip-flops. Part of being a member of your community means dressing like them. You want to fit in, which is hard enough when protocol puts you up on a pedestal.

Sometimes it is OK to dress down and wear jeans and a t-shirt – as long as you are dressing like your audience. If you are in anyway worried, dress one step further up the smartness scale than them. If you really aren't sure contact the organisers. Just never wear black tie or fancy dress unless you are specifically requested to. Don't stand out in the wrong way.

Gone are the days when mayors wore formal morning dress to most events. Trust me, those days really are gone. You have my permission to dress down when appropriate.

Robes

Robes can appear as a barrier between people and civic leaders. There are events where you will have to wear them, if everyone else on the council is wearing them then you will look out of place if you don't. You will have your own take on it but don't ignore the advice of your civic team.

You might want to wear your robes when you are going to be talking a lot about the history of the role, such as on school visits. But don't just assume that you can. Consult your civic team and find out what the policy is. This will avoid disappointment and a stern lecture about robes not being dressing-up clothes.

The chain

The chain helps. It instantly identifies you. It makes it easier for people to say hello to you. It is like a giant sign saying please chat to me. Again, there will be local rules regarding your chain. Consult your civic team to find out what they expect of you. It is an honour to wear your chain as it is an important part of the history of your community. Whatever you do, look after it.

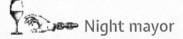 Night mayor

A mayor left their chain in their twin town. They got it back but many years later people are still telling the story about the mayor who left the chain in the twin town. Don't be that mayor.

A non-political role

You have figured out that you are taking on a non-political one. You shouldn't need reminding that you must not use the role as a platform for campaigning.

But it can be complicated. Sometimes members of the public will not respect your neutrality; sometimes they just hear you are a politician and expect you to be political. Sometimes you need to work with people who have totally different political opinions. It is worth spending a moment or two considering the following questions.

How non-political is non-political?

- At what point will you stop talking about politics while at engagements?

- Are there any party-political issues on your council that could get in the way?

- Are you comfortable promoting what your council is doing if you aren't a member of the ruling party?

- If you are working closely with people from other parties how comfortable will you be?

Interviewing a previous incumbent

Once you have filled out the calendar as much as you can, thought about your appointments, reviewed the associated roles and pondered all the rest of it then you will need to ensure that you haven't missed anything. The best way to do this is to check with someone who has done the job.

You will need to find a civic leader that has recently left office. It doesn't have to be the last holder of the office but they shouldn't have stood down too long ago. Things change. This discussion will be much more productive if it is informal. Doubtless they will want to reminisce. Doubtless they will tell you how great it was. Try to steer the conversation onto your questions.

Fact-finding mission

- What events are significant in themselves – for example: Remembrance Sunday?

- What events involve lots of work?

- When are the quiet points during the year?

- What is missing from the diary exercise?

- Were there any issues with the civic team?

- Was the diary well organised?

- Are any of the associated roles time-consuming?

- Are there any other questions that you have?

Should you talk to the current civic leader?

You could do. If they have time. Part of being a civic leader is helping the next wave to excel. Maybe they don't recognise that and they don't think it is the best use of their precious time. There is only one way to find out.

Something to build on

You should be paying attention to what the current mayor is doing. You should ask yourself the following questions:

- What are they doing well?

- What are they doing that you can build on?

- What has the media been particularly interested in?

- What has gone down well online?

- Which council projects have they successfully championed?

Most important of all:

- How can you replicate these successes?

The chances are that you can answer those questions without speaking to them. If you have a few questions for them it may be better if you grab them for five minutes next time you see them or give them a call rather than trying to meet up with them.

What opportunities are there?

What is on the horizon

You should have an idea of what your council will be doing over the next few years. Is there anything that you can see looming that could be an opportunity to enhance your year in office? Could something in the future help enhance the message that you want to spread? Are there any significant anniversaries coming up?

 Twenty-first century mayor

Peter Green, Mayor of Abingdon, realised that he would take office during the anniversary of the town's charter. Through tenacity and hard work he made the celebrations happen. The highlight was a royal visit. He made the anniversary and the anniversary made his year.

Not just anniversaries

Councils do much more than celebrate anniversaries. Maybe your council has a significant project that will finish and you can help celebrate while you are in office? Maybe there will be major changes to services that you can help promote? Even the increase in devolved powers presents an opportunity for civic leaders. How are you going to get involved?

If you aren't sure what's coming up ask other councillors what they see on the horizon. They should give you some good ideas.

Strategic plan

Your council will have strategic objectives and they will be outlined in a document. You may have helped to create yours; at the very least you should have read it.

It is a good time to re-read it. It will help if you can relate what you are hoping to achieve to the aims of the council. This will mean you get support from councillors and senior staff. Ultimately, there is a lot of pressure on council budgets. If you are seen to be supporting the council's long term goals then there is a reason for funding your office.

Why you need to build relationships

Meeting the movers and shakers

You are going to meet with senior councillors and staff and on the face of it this is a simple fact-finding mission. But that is only the surface. Each meeting is an opportunity to start, improve or cement a relationship.

Building relationships

> **Quick Win**
>
> Look through the strategic plan. Which area most interests you? How can your time in office enhance that?

The best way of building relationships is by turning up and doing what you say you are going to do. You should have been doing that throughout your time as councillor. If you have then you are in a good position. If not, get visible and busy.

Where are you going with these relationships?

Good relationships are what will make your time on office a success. Ultimately, you are building relationships for two reasons: clarity and support.

Clarity

You are going to have to make sure that your expectations are the same as the council's, you don't need to do that now but it will be part of your aims soon. You will need to talk with senior councillors and staff to make sure that they aren't going to object to what you are trying to do. It is simple. If influential people on your council are going to block your plans you need to know sooner rather than later. You won't know about their objections if you don't have a relationship with them.

Support

You will need guidance and advice. You will need information and resources. Occasionally you will even need a good hug. Different people in your council can offer different combinations of these. There is a lot of support open to you if you can develop the relationships to access it.

So how do you work out where to start?

Everyone sits somewhere on the relationship/influence axis. Some people are better known to you so they are higher on the relationship side,

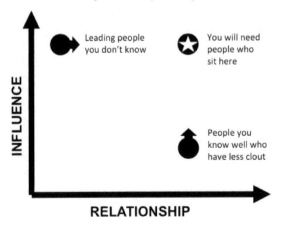

some people are more influential so they are further up the other axis. When you take office you will need to have a selection of people in the sweet spot.

It is not that now you should only talk to people with power it is simply that this exercise is about gauging the opinions of the people who have influence on your council. But you can't affect how influential the people you have relationships with are so you must develop relationships with people who are influential. Keep this in mind as you progress through the exercises that follow.

Take a notebook

When you meet with senior councillors and staff you will need to take notes. Not only will this make a useful record but it will also make them see that you are serious and that you truly value their opinion.

Keep your eyes peeled

The purpose of this information-gathering process, is to find opportunities not to spot problems. However, if you do see some pitfalls don't ignore them. Make a quick note of anything that could derail your plans. This could be a lack of staff support or the attitude of your fellow councillors. Likewise, you may find that someone has already tried to implement a project that you wanted to without success.

Who you need to meet

There is no simple answer to who you should speak to as there are many variables. It depends on how your council works and who you have relationships with. But it isn't a good idea to start with the CEO you have barely meet. That won't be an easy meeting. Start by thinking about where the following people sit on the relationship/influence axis:

- Your political group leader

- The council leader

- The portfolio holders or cabinet members

- The chief executive or town clerk

- The head of the directorate that the civic office is a part of

For the next fact- inding mission you will only need to meet one or two of them. It is worth keeping the relationship/influence axis in mind, though, if you are interacting with these people during your council business remember that sooner or later you will need to talk to them about your plans. How can you improve your relationship?

Who to talk to first

For now you are going to concentrate on senior councillors. There will be time to consider the staff later.

The leader of the council

In an ideal world you will go straight to the council leader because you have already got a quality relationship. Your world might be ideal, it might not. If you don't feel comfortable meeting with the leader then you should meet with the most senior councillor that you can. You want a general overview of the top of the council. Just bear in mind that any cabinet member may have their own agenda. They will try to push things from their portfolio.

You need to look for opportunities and things to build on. Senior councillors should be well briefed on what will be coming up and how this might fit with your aims. They will also have a good idea of what message the council is trying to promote. They can help you make sure what you are doing is of real benefit to the council.

Fact-finding mission

- What projects are coming up?

- What should be the focus of your time in office?

- What should you tell people about?

- What is the council's big issue?

- What are people asking about?

- How can you support the council's strategic aims?

- Is there anything else you would like to know?

You may have noticed that these questions are centred around how you can help them, not how they can help you. This will help you to serve your council but it will also help build a solid relationship. They will be pleased that you are trying to deliver value for the council.

If they are keen to hear what you want to do there is no harm in telling them. Just be sure that you talk about things that you *might* do, not what you're *going* to do. Suggestions are better received than dogmatic statements of intent.

Reflect on what you have found out

You have covered a lot of ground. Don't worry if you can't get it all done in the next two days. Take some time but get it done. And don't worry if you can't digest it all at once. In time you will start to understand how what you have found out can fit into your plans.

What to do now

Your civic team
- Meet them. Make sure you are happy with what they do. Specifically make sure you are clear about how the relationship will work throughout your time in office.

Have you got a clear idea of what the year will look like?
- Make sure you understand how the year will pan out.

Who will be your chaplain?
- If you think it will be a simple appointment check with the civic office. If you don't start asking the opinions of your political group and senior councillors.

What opportunities are there?

- Get talking, get researching and try to uncover any interesting areas that could be incorporate into your plan.

Read your council's strategic plan

- Pay attention to how you can contribute to the policy objectives.

Have you built some relationships?

- You should meet with at least one senior councillor, preferably two.

The Genial Host

"Do not concern yourself with people who talk about you, concern yourself with people who talk with you".

Mark Harris, Mayor of Cirencester 2015-2016

It is about people

You are really starting to make some headway. It is exciting finally to get into the nitty gritty of the role you are going to undertake. It is great to start to feel that it is real. Of course, it is also worrying, you are starting to see exactly how much you have to do. But that is balanced out by the flashes of what you could achieve, those glimpses of what your year could be.

Now you are going to look at meeting people. It is an important subject because everything you are going to achieve while in office will come from the relationships you build. Those relationships have got to start somewhere. Naturally it is an area you could have some concerns about. Going into a room full of strangers is scary. It is hard making conversation. It is difficult remembering people's names. If that worries you then you are perfectly normal.

Just remember that people want to meet you. They feel honoured to meet civic leaders and when you do meet them and make them feel special that is when you begin to have an impact. Each meeting is full of potential because it is people who will turn your dreams into reality.

The genial host

Why you are always the host

- Why you always need to put people first.

How to make someone feel like they are the only person in the room

- This is at the heart of everything you want to achieve.

How to make conversation with anyone
- A few tricks of the engagement trade.

Why it is important to remember people
- Names and faces can be hard to recollect, but you can make it easier.

How to chair a meeting
- A seriously useful skill, particularly for council chairs.

How to prepare for a full council meeting
- A quick guide to smooth your way into the big meetings.

Who will help you with full council
- You need advice on this, who is going to provide it?

Why you are always the host

Being asked to attend an event seems very different from organising one, but if you want to engage as many people as possible you shouldn't treat attending and organising differently. If you adopt the attitude that you are always the host then people will respond well to you. You don't need to take over but applying some of the principles of hosting an event will help you come across as a generous and friendly person.

Get into the habit of introducing people. If you think that two people don't know each other, introduce them. The probable outcome will be they have someone new to talk to. But you never know what might come from a chance meeting.

You should make sure that people are comfortable. You don't have to fuss but you should never miss a chance to demonstrate your generosity. If you are going to the buffet ask the people you're talking to if they want to come. This even works if you are going to talk to someone: ask the person you're currently talking to if they want to accompany you. You may want to do the same thing with drinks but it will get expensive if the bar isn't free.

By making sure that people are enjoying themselves you are enhancing their experience of the event. But it also makes you seem generous and confident.

How to make someone feel like they are the only person in the room

It is hard

To be blunt, meeting new people is scary, making small talk can be boring and remembering names is hard. Yet it is worth making the effort because meeting new people is the start of having an impact on your community.

In the next few pages you won't be able to assuage all your fears but there will be some tips about making people feel special. More importantly there will be some techniques that will make you feel more confident. Which will really help because you will spend a lot of time meeting people. If you can get more comfortable with that you are more than half way there.

Make them feel important

It doesn't matter which great leader you are talking about – Mandela, Obama or Churchill, people who meet them all say the same thing. When they talk to you it feels like you are the only person in the room. Part of what makes them great is their ability to make people feel important. That is what you need to aspire to.

Meeting a civic leader should be a big thing. It should be special; it should be memorable. But how do you achieve that? How do you make sure that meeting you is a standout experience?

It is not as difficult as you might think. All you need to do is be interested rather than trying to be interesting. It should be about them. Concentrate on showing them you are pleased to meet them rather than expecting them to be pleased to meet you. Talk about who they are and what they do. Ask them questions. If you focus on them they will feel like they are the only person in the world.

Other than that, the only thing you need to do is enjoy yourself. If you are not having fun then how do you expect your guests to have fun? The worst thing in the world is to meet someone who is bored and disinterested. Enjoy yourself!

How to make conversation with anyone

Relationships develop along predictable lines. They start with small talk, then progress to the exchange of information, then move to an exchange of opinion. They may then progress to an exchange of emotions. It is important to get this development in the right order.

You get nervous when you meet people who are too keen to exchange opinions or emotion. They have broken the unwritten rules of relationships. You want people to build up a conversation from small, easily digestible pieces, like their journey here or the weather. That is the point of small talk, it should be light opening remarks. Once they have done that you might let them tell us something about themselves. After that you may be ready for opinions and emotions. It is essential to master small talk because that is where engagement starts.

Small Talk

You may wonder how to start these conversations. After all, talking about something small is a bit vague. It helps if you have a wide selection of questions to ask. There are two tactics for coming up with questions: think like a hairdresser or ask about the organisation.

What you can learn from hairdressers

If you haven't already worked this out, go and get a haircut. Hairdressers are experts at starting conversations and they do it almost entirely by asking questions. Typically, they will open with something like this:

- How was your journey?
- What have you been doing today?
- Do you have any plans for the weekend?
- Are you going on holiday?
- What do you think of the weather?

None of it is earth-shattering but you don't want to start a conversation with anything profound. It is all small stuff.

Ask about the organisation

Another great way to get people talking is to discuss the group running the event. There are many questions that you can ask:

- What is your role in the organisation?

- How long have you been involved?

- What attracted you to the organisation?

- What are the aims of the organisation?

- Who is the organisation trying to help?

- How does the organisation want to develop?

By the end of the event you will be a regular expert on the group. By the end of the year you will know more about your community than just about anyone else.

You will wish you hadn't asked

There are some areas you should be wary about mentioning. People are sometimes unhappy talking about their families or their jobs. This might seem strange because people are always asking about your family or your job, but it doesn't mean it is a great idea. What if you ask someone who has recently been bereaved about their family? Or someone who has just been made redundant about their job? It is not worth the risk.

> **Quick Win**
>
> Next time you meet someone try thinking like a hairdresser. Ask them a mundane question and see where it takes you.

> **Quick Win**
>
> Next time you meet someone try asking them about the event you are at. See how much you can learn.

Why it is important to remember people

What is in a name

Getting people's names right is important. But you know that. At some point in your life someone will have got your name wrong. It makes you feel that they don't have much regard for you. They can't think much of you if they can't even remember your name.

Many people claim to be bad at remembering names. This is often because they are bad at listening to people's names. In fairness, many people don't help you out. What you want to concentrate on is remembering their first name. How do they introduce themselves? The name's Bond, James Bond. The trick is to forget the Bond and concentrate on the James.

What if you can't remember their name?

If you've been talking to someone as if you know them but you can't remember their name you could end up in a sticky situation. If you can't remember someone's name it is better to ask straight away.

As you have met them before you will remember something about them. Open with what you can remember and then ask for clarification of their name. Something along the lines of: "we met at the Lion's Club, what was your name again?" You have proved that they are important enough for you to remember them. They will assume, rightly, that you meet a lot of people and can't be expected to remember everyone's name.

It comes down to a simple point. You are trying to make people feel special. Are they special enough that you remember their name?

Don't just remember names, remember people

You want to achieve a lot during your time in office. You will need to build many relationships to do that. When you are at events you will meet people that can help you. Sometimes it is obvious that they can help you. Sometimes it is only much later that you work this out.

Either way it is important to remember the people that you meet, what they do and how to get in touch with them.

Don't talk business now

When you have meet someone that could help you it is tempting to launch into a long conversation about what they can do for you. Tempting, but not a good idea. You have come to this event to meet people, get to know an organisation, present an award or a thousand other reasons. You have not come to plan your next event.

The sensible thing to do is to ask the person concerned if you can get in touch with them. Get their business card and agree a time to follow up. That way you can concentrate on engaging everyone else.

Business Cards

You should be issued with some official cards by your council. As councils tend not to be great at design you might want to get your own printed. These should have your office details on rather than your personal details. All engagements must go through your office. You should be generous with your cards and hand them out as often as possible. It is another great way of making people feel special.

Once you have given someone your card they will usually give you theirs. It is important to keep hold of these business cards and record them in some way. You could input them into a contact management system. There are many online tools which will help you do this. You could collect all the cards from an event in a sealer bag and record them in batches. You may even be able to get a little help with the data entry.

LinkedIn

The other great way to keep track of people is LinkedIn. LinkedIn is a business network, you will cover it more in a later chapter. In essence it works like Facebook but it is more professional. If you know their full name you may find them but it is easier if you know where they live and work too. You can then ask them to connect and you will be able to contact them when you need to.

Connecting with people on LinkedIn after an event is time well spent. Think of it as a giant portable address book.

How to chair a meeting

You the chair

You are going to be chairing meetings and you may as well get it right. Full council probably isn't the only meeting that you will have to chair; there will almost certainly be an amount of showpiece chairing. This involves heading prestigious meeting for your council or chairing AGMs of local charities and organisation. Both types of meeting will put you on show.

Listen, think, speak – in that order.

What you say is way down the list. If you aren't thinking you will talk rubbish. If you aren't listening, you will talk irrelevant rubbish. Listen, think, speak – in that order.

Always the host

When you are the chair it pays to act as the host too. You should welcome people as they arrive. You should make sure no-one is left out of the conversation before the meeting begins. You should be genial and smile when you ask people to speak. You should maintain eye contact and nod to show you are listening. Perhaps most important of all you should always say thank you to the participants.

Chairing tactics

If you aren't familiar with your council's standing orders then you should get to know them. It is not always obvious but council meetings are governed by the standing orders. You should expect all councillors to respect the rules and respect the chair.

Meetings can drag so it is important to keep things moving. As the chair, you are supposed to be neutral so it isn't appropriate to just blurt out "get a move on!" The way to get things moving is through the intelligent use of questions. The right question can be used to speed up progress in the following ways:

- Closed questions, which must be answered with a yes or no, can help people get to the point.

- Open questions, which can't be answered with yes or no, can be used to elicit the opinion of someone who is struggling to take part in the discussion.

- You can rephrase or restate the opinion of the room as a question. This can help bring people to a resolution.

- Commands can be phrased as a question, such as 'shouldn't we return to the original issue?'. This can help people return to the subject at hand.

Don't be tempted to turn into some sort of dictator. You can ask questions but remember you are also the host.

Some dilemmas for potential chairs

You will find yourself in many situations. Here are a few to make you think about what you would do when chairing gets tough. Think about how you might use questions and your hosting skills to help.

Meeting one

The meeting is dragging on. A member who tends to go on has stood to speak about a small item right at the end. They immediately digress onto their pet topic. They have been speaking for several minutes and show no sign of stopping. What do you do?

Meeting two

A councillor is aggressive in their response to someone who disagrees with them. They become increasingly aggressive and rude. They start swearing. What do you do?

Meeting three

A robust debate has been going on about an issue concerning an area of your community. The ward member, who is shy, has not asked to speak.

What do you do?

Meeting four

A member of the public has asked a question of a cabinet member. The person begins by reading the question as it is asked but then they start digressing. What do you do?

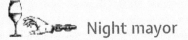 Night mayor

Mayor of Siliguri, Ashok Bhattacharya, was hit on the head by a mic stand thrown at him during a particularly aggressive debate in an Indian council meeting. Keep your councillors in check!

Point of order

There is no such thing as a point of order. It is a device used by naughty councillors who are trying to disrupt the meeting or advance their own agenda. Check your standing orders. If anyone tries to make a point of order, ask them which subsection of the standing orders they think has been incorrectly applied. That does the trick.

Practice makes improvement

The more you chair meetings the better you will get at it. Chairing is a very specific skill and one you can't really develop in any other role. In theory it should be easy for you to learn these skills. Your council has many meetings and they all need chairing – why aren't they helping you to get some experience?

Unless your council has a training plan you will have to develop your own way of getting prepared. In an ideal world you would chair a small committee for a year and then move up to a larger group. Having chaired that for a year or two you would be ready to take the step up to full council. If you don't have two or three years try to get as much experience as you can. Here are some things to think about:

- Can you find a council committee to chair?

- What organisations do you belong to that might be able to offer you opportunities?

- Could you volunteer specifically for a role to get some experience?

- Would your team benefit from have a meeting that you could chair?

If you only have a few chances, use them wisely. Prepare properly. Keep up with what is going on. Think about what went well and what could be improved. If possible, get someone at the meeting to give you feedback.

How to prepare for a full council meeting

Before the meeting

As soon as the agenda is available you need to familiarise yourself with it. Read it through a couple of times and make notes of anything you don't understand or need to follow up.

It is essential that you meet with a senior member of staff. You can work out who shortly. They should have the knowledge, experience and insight to foresee potential problems. Make lots of notes when you meet them. If you need to ask the portfolio holders or the council leader any questions make sure you do so in plenty of time. In fact, your council may organise a meeting for you, senior officers and the leader.

Once you have spoken to people you will have all the information you need to prepare a folder for the meeting. Copy up your notes neatly onto a clean agenda. Make sure you hole-punch everything and put it into a folder. Don't try to use a stapled agenda. It is much easier to keep your place if you only need to turn the page.

You will also need to check the agenda for anything that you will need to talk about. This may be as simple as your announcements or you may want to report some information on a relevant organisation or project. Make sure you have made notes to remind yourself where to add these. Add a page of notes if you need more detail or you don't think you will be able to remember exactly what to say.

Just because you have notes doesn't mean you shouldn't practice. Take a little time to make sure you are comfortable with everything you need to say. Once everything is done check through it one last time.

At the meeting

It is worth having a quick chat with the senior officer and the council leader immediately before the meeting. This gives you a chance to find out if anything has changed last minute. You wouldn't want any nasty surprises to derail your careful preparation.

Once the meeting starts you only have one job to do. Concentrate. If you don't keep up with what is going on the meeting won't stay on track. The skill of chairing is being able to keep your ears on what is being said, your eyes on the agenda and your brain on what you are going to say next. With practice, you can develop the skill of listening to the present while planning the future and this will mean that your meetings will flow nicely.

In addition to knowing the agenda you will need to know the people. Use your knowledge of the councillor's personalities to manage their contributions to the meeting. Try to anticipate what might come up. There is a lot to learn which is why it is important to get some practice.

Who will help you with full council?

Preparation for full council meetings is a big thing but you are not alone. Arrange to chat about it with a senior staff member. Think back to the relationship/influence axis and decide which senior staff member is most appropriate and book a meeting.

It is the relationship that counts

The best approach is to ask them for help. Kick off by asking them how they can help you prepare for full council. If you explain that you know it is important and you know you will need some guidance you will get off to a good start. Tell them about anything that you are worried about and they will try to help.

Once you have established a relationship there is lots of other information you need to know.

Fact Finding Mission

- Are there any big projects coming up that you need to know about?

- What issues are people talking about?

- Which of the council's messages should you share?

- Will any special occasions fall in your year?

- If you have a problem who should you talk to?

In the unlikely event that there isn't anyone who is ready to help you prepare then you should start complaining to the most influential person you have managed to build a relationship with. It is important that you are prepared for full council and you will need help.

Reflect on what you have found out

By now you should have met with your civic team and some senior councillors, or at least arranged to. It is important that you get these underway as you now have another meeting to arrange.

Take a moment to reflect on what you have learnt. Have you identified any great opportunities? Have you found out the boundaries of the support you are going to get? Are you happy with it? Are there more things you would like to know? Are you getting excited? You should be because you are making important headway.

What to do next

Practice making conversation with people you have never meet

- Think about the questions you could ask. Think about how you can make them feel special. Most of all practice.

Keep a record of people you meet

- Try out LinkedIn if you don't use it already. Make sure you have a way of tracking the people who could help you.

Practice your chairing skills

- Even if you have a lot of experience you can always hone your skills. Make your own opportunities if you must.

Meet with a senior member of the council's staff

- Get the questions answered and begin to build relationships.

VISION

Community is the New Charity

"If you continue to take without putting something back – like a well of water – it will go dry".

Gbola Adeleke, Mayor of Dacorum 2015-2016

Moving forward

You are five chapters in, the opportunities and ideas are coming thick and fast. It is an exciting time as your imagination is on fire and you can really see the potential of the opportunity in front of you. Doubtless, you are also feeling the demands of all that thinking, researching and talking, maybe a few exercises have slipped because you haven't quite got round to them. Make sure you do find the time because these exercises are the ones that will really get you to the exhilarating times you can see in the distance.

You joined the council to make a difference to your community and you are about to take a look at how you can do that. This is by far the most satisfying part of being a civic leader, having a real impact on the community. It is something to be proud of. Of course it is not easy. It will involve you breaking out and doing new things. Taking a new direction is always a challenge. It would not be surprising if you started to wonder if you shouldn't just get back on the well-trodden path.

You need to remember that taking the right path – not the obvious path – is how you make a difference. The benefits of creating that lasting impact in your community are huge. You live there, you will see what you have done again and again. For the rest of your life, the people who you have touched will remind you of the great work you have done.

Community is the new charity

Do you want to raise money for charity?

- You are generous, you like charity but is it the right thing to do with this opportunity?

What could you do instead?

- You don't have to be a fundraising machine, here is an idea of something else you could do.

What is your community strategy?

- It is your community, how are you going to improve it?

What is your charity strategy?

- It is time to get clear about what you are going to do to help.

Who will help you?

- You achieve so much more when you have a good team behind you.

How does this fit into your time in office?

- It is all important but it has still got to fit into your overall plan for your time in office.

Do you want to raise money for charity?

Why civic leaders fund raise

It might seem strange but there is no legal obligation for civic leaders to raise funds for charity. It appears to be such an integral part of what they do, but it is nothing more than tradition that keeps it going.

It seems as if one mayor raises money so the next one feels they should. Then the next one feels they should and so on. The appropriate way to think of it is as baggage that comes with the office. It is done because it has always been done and that is no reason at all.

You do not have to

It is completely up to you whether you want to do any charity work. I will just say that again: you *do not* have to raise money for charity. You should seriously consider whether you have the time and energy to mount a major fundraising campaign during the busiest year of your life.

Pause for a moment and think.

Is it a priority for you?

It may feel strange to think about not doing something that is so associated with mayors and council chairs.

Take a few moments to think about the following questions:

- How much motivation do you have for charity work?

- Are you fired up to get through the difficult times?

- How much of your own money do you want to put into raising cash for good causes?

- Do you have time not just for engagements and admin but also for trudging round shops trying to drum up raffle prizes?

Is it a priority for your council?

A couple of chapters ago you should have had a look at your council's strategic plan. Given that they aren't the most exciting things in the world maybe you didn't get around to it. But now you really should get hold of a copy. List the heading for your council's four or five main areas of work:

1 ....

2 ....

3 ....

4 ....

5 ....

Your council has a lot of things it's legally bound to do. These days it will have many things that it is trying to achieve and only a limited budget with which to achieve them. Use the following questions to think about where charity work would sit within those priorities.

- Does raising money for charity contribute to your council's aims?

- Your office is funded by taxpayer's money. Should it be used to raise money for a charity of your choosing?

- Does your council have more pressing issues that you could help with?

- Are there more important things you could do for your community than raise funds?

What could you do instead?

If you are starting to think you don't want to do any charity work, that is OK. If you never had much enthusiasm for it, that is OK. If you think you could better spend your time, that is OK.

Every civic leader must find their own path. If yours isn't about charity work, then that is 100% fine. It does not make you a bad person. You have a limited amount of time. You have a limited amount of energy. Your council has limited resources. You must prioritise. You must put your effort into what you care about. Make a difference there; don't try to spread yourself across everything.

Just to make this totally clear: it is perfectly acceptable not to do any charity work.

Forget charity

That said, you can't very well announce to all and sundry that you don't like charity. It doesn't matter how well you put it – that is not going to sound good. What do you do?

You should nominate a single charity, but you don't have to do any fundraising for it. The good news is other people may well do that for you.

There may be events that will be organised without much input from you. You will also find that random people will give you money for your charity. At the end of the year you will have raised some money for your chosen cause while still concentrating on what you want to do. Everyone wins.

The bad news is you should still need to read the rest of this chapter and spend a bit of time finding out what the existing charity set-up is.

What could you do instead? Many civic leaders put their efforts into raising money because they see it as a way they can have an impact. It is time that effort got channelled into creating initiatives to improve communities. This will have a far greater impact than raising money that is often not even spent locally. Community is the new charity.

Take another look at your council's strategic plan

It would be surprising if your strategic plan involved rising money for charity. It would be equally surprising if it *didn't* mention community. How can you channel the energy and effort that has been used to raise funds for charity in the past into improving your community?

 ### Twenty-first century mayor

Fiasal Rashid, Mayor of Warrington, organised an event called Breaking Down Barriers. It brought together many groups from his community to talk about their shared humanity. It was very popular because it caught the mood of the time. It was very powerful because it showed different areas of the community how much they had in common.

Ask yourself these questions:

- What would you be prouder of, a glitzy ball or an event that brought your community closer together?

- How can you change existing charity events to make them more community-focused?

- What is your community crying out for? How can you provide it?

- How can what you want to do tie in with your council's community aims?

Putting your community at the heart of your vision and your year can have a real impact. That really would be something to be proud of.

What is your community strategy?

It is great coming up with new events and initiatives that enhance your community. There is nothing wrong with doing that – just try not to get too carried away. Some civic leaders have enough plans for five years in office. One big idea or a couple of smaller ones is enough. Incorporate them into your vision, put them into action and make a difference.

Before you start to develop new events, have you thought about how you can reimagine charity events as community events?

What have you inherited?

The first thing you need to do is take a long hard look at the events that happen every year. Is there a charity ball, a curry evening, a quiz or carol concert? You will need to find out as much as you can about these events.

The questions below should help.

- How much money does the event raise?

- How much effort does it take to organise?

- Are they being done because they always have been?

- Do people enjoy these events?

- Do these events contribute anything to the mission of the council?

You might find that there are some long-standing charity events that are well run and well attended. In which case let them carry on.

You may find events that aren't very good. You should probably cancel them and concentrate your efforts elsewhere. This may cause complaints: doubtless some people are fond of the annual tiddlywinks match. They might be swayed by a logical argument, but sometimes you need to keep an event against your better judgement. In this case there are two ways you can re-imagine it.

Make it an event for the community

The best way to breathe life into a tired event, is to refocus it as a community occasion. If the event has a clear purpose that furthers your council's strategic aims then it is appropriate for your civic team to work on it. If it's only benefit is raising money then it needs to raise a lot of money: if it has a community benefit then it only needs to break even. Here are some ideas for refocusing events:

- A gala dinner for community champions rather than a charity ball

- A challenge that's about promoting a cause rather than raising money

- An evening of entertainment that brings together different sections of the community rather than a concert to raise money

- A quiz night where each round promotes a different local business

- A week of community events rather than a week of charity events

There are many ways you could refresh your current charity events. The only limit is your imagination.

Make it more profitable

If you are keeping a charity event that hasn't performed well it will need to start raising more money. There is a simple rule in business: if you want to make more money you need to either reduce expenditure, raise prices or sell more. You will need to look at your options with either the event's organising team or your charity committee.

What else do you want to do?

You are probably bursting with ideas and the possibilities are endless. Whether you are focusing on community, charity or another area it is wise to plan something to get things going.

Start with a bang

Some civic leaders plan a spectacular start to their year, like a parachute jump. It is a great kick off: it gets press coverage and it gives the fundraising team a boost. How are you going to start with a bang? What will be your first attention-grabbing event?

Catch their attention

Whatever you are trying to achieve, some buzz in the press, on the street and on social media will help. Try to make your event sound interesting and not run-of-the-mill. Something that is a big personal challenge will interest people. Something unusual is guaranteed to get people talking. Don't fear raising an eyebrow or two. There are many things that people won't expect a civic leader to do – play on that.

 Twenty-first century mayor

Toby Eliot, Mayor of Frome, walked a mile. Not so impressive, except he did it in high heels. His surprising event raised money but more importantly it raised the profile of the white ribbon campaign to end male violence against women.

How much is too much?

You should be getting excited about the opportunity to create new events. Excitement is great. It is just sometimes it is worth remembering that you only have a year. Don't fall into the trap of trying to do too much: even one event a month is a lot.

Dairy check

Jot down your ideas on this calendar and make sure they are spaced out. If you have a concentration of events at one time, move them around. It is better not to move well-established events as it will dent ticket sales.

YEAR PLANNER

MAY	JUNE	JULY

AUGUST	SEPTEMBER	OCTOBER

NOVEMBER	DECEMBER	JANUARY

FEBRUARY	MARCH	APRIL

What is your charity strategy?

Choosing the right partner

If you are going to be doing any charity work the first thing you should do is pick a charity partner. You may have some ideas but it is worth taking a moment to think about who is right for you.

There is a strong argument for picking local charities. If there is any suggestion that you are using council resources for charity work it seems sensible that it is for a local cause. At least there is some benefit to the community. In fact, your council probably supports many charities that are either service providers or recipients of grants. It makes sense to support one of these groups.

Some civic leaders pick multiple charities. This is fine but only if you are doing it for the right reasons. Don't do it because that is what people in the past have done, particularly if you know of a local charity that needs the money.

 **Night mayor**

One mayor was constantly complaining that their events weren't being supported by their charity. The charity was large and had many members locally. They thought that the charity should be providing people to help at their events. Never pick a charity because you think they can help your fundraising efforts. Sometimes they can. Sometimes they can't. Remember that you're trying to help them, not the other way around.

Who will help you?

The charity committee

Your council may have a well-developed fundraising strategy that has been honed over the years. Then again it may not. If you don't have a charity committee you should set one up. This will take a lot of work and will need to be your focus for a while but it is worth doing.

 **Twenty-first century mayor**

In Canterbury the fundraising is handled by Lady Mayoress' Charity. It is run by an independent board of trustees that approve what is done. It has a separate legal identity so there can be no question that the council is spending tax payer's money on fundraising.

You need a charity committee for two good reasons. Firstly, it takes the burden of fundraising away from your civic team. Running a fundraising campaign is not a good use of officer time and taxpayers' money. A charity committee should be made up of volunteers, which would eliminate this problem. Secondly, you are going to be busy and won't have the time to run a campaign. The charity committee should.

The first thing to do is to appoint a committee chair. This should be someone that you know, like and trust. They should be the go-to person for every part of your fundraising campaign. You should be happy for them to take control of the project. Yes, they will expect your input but they should be in charge.

Once you have a chair you should start to recruit people to fill the committee. Around ten is about right. Here are some ideas for people you could recruit:

- Representatives of the charities you support

- Your chaplain

- Your deputy

- People with useful skills such as design or social media

- Hard-working and keen friends of yours

- Council employees that are willing to help away from work time

- Any suggestions that your committee chair has

Finally you should consider creating a legal identity for this committee. The process of registering a charity can be complex but it is possible. You will need a documented structure and a charitable purpose that is for the public benefit. This takes any fundraising completely away from the council and with a dedicated committee, it takes it away from you too.

You can find out more about registering a charity from www.gov.uk.

How does this fit into your time in office?

Don't forget if you are committing to spending a lot of time and effort on charity work it is time you can't spend on something else. That is a big reason you should think whether it is at the core of what you want to do. What else could you achieve with that time? I'm not telling you not to do any fundraising. I'm asking you to think hard about it.

 Night mayor

A mayor organised a charity ball. The council covered the cost of printing the posters, mailing out invites, selling the tickets and a lot of staff-time to put everything together. The ball made £200. Could you justify that to a voter on the doorstep?

If you couldn't justify spending taxpayer's money on a poorly performing charity event to a voter then you should think about whether it is right for civic leaders to use their time and their council's resources to raise money.

Over to you

Ultimately, if you are going to spend time on something – be it charity work or bringing your community closer together – it needs to be a part of your vision for your time in office. It is nearly time to make a start developing your vision, because a solid vision will help you maximise your impact.

What to do next

Do you want to raise money for charity?

- It is OK if you do not. Plan how you are going to handle this without making yourself look like a miser.

How do you plan to have an impact on your community?

- Consider changing charity events into community events. But most of all try to harness the energy that is usually used to fundraise to leave a lasting impression on your community.

You need help

- Your charity efforts should not take up the civic team's time. Make sure you have a chairperson to spearhead the efforts and support them with a committee. Consider giving it a legal identity.

What events will you be doing

- Find out what already exists. If it isn't performing reduce costs, increase sales or cut it. Think about what else you want to do particularly things that will grab attention.

Fit it into your vision

- Whether you are doing community work or fundraising it needs to be a part of your vision. Only do it if it is part of the change you want to create.

Developing Your Vision

The Mayor plays on the "big pitch" for a year and should seek to score some big goals!

Paul Millward, Chair of the National Association of Civic Officers

Seeing the changes

By now you will have come across unforeseen opportunities and unexpected ideas. This is great. These are the new and innovative concepts you need to bring to your office. But the unexpected can be troubling. Maybe some of your plans seem to have derailed. Maybe you are not so sure about something that you thought was straightforward. That is OK. Just remember that the unexpected often turns out to have the biggest impact. Surprise yourself and surprise your community.

You are now in a much better position to develop your vision and a vision will really help you. You will achieve much more if you are clear on what you are trying to do. Clarity of purpose will save you a lot of time. Of course getting to that point is difficult. Developing a vision is difficult. It won't come straight away, you will need to wrestle with it and refine it. Clarity is hard.

Still a clear vision will repay you many times over. It will give you a starting point for speeches and interviews by giving you the building blocks of a message when you don't have much time to prepare. But more than that, it will let you communicate what you want to achieve to all the people that want to help you and follow you. If you can tell people they can help you.

Developing your vision

What do you want to do?
- By now you should be bursting with ideas about what you want to achieve.

What do you have to do?
- You should also have a good idea about what your obliged to do.

Do you have what you need to do them?

- Time, skills and support are all precious resources, do you have enough?

What are your core values?

- It is important to get clear about the principles that will guide you while in office.

What is your vision?

- A little scary, a little exciting, it is time to begin a vision of your own.

What do you want to do?

What do you want to see?

You are going to begin the process of developing your vision statement. When you have finished it will be at the heart of what you will do while in office. You are not going to write a list of things to do, you will do that in the planning phase but for now you are going to look at what you want to achieve.

The key to a vision statement is that it is about what the world will be like when you have finished, it describes the change you are going to create. It is the impact you are going to have in a nutshell.

What would you do if you had no constraints?

Look back to almost the first exercise, "what kind of a civic leader are you going to be?" Take a minute or two to look through your answers and reflect on them. Keep those thought in your mind when you complete the next exercise.

You are going to write a list of things you would like to achieve while in office. When you have finished it will have thirty ideas on it. That is a big number. That is the point. You are going to have to think hard to come up with that many ideas. Somewhere amongst all that free-thinking you will find a few gems. There are no limitations – write down whatever you like. More importantly there are no bad ideas.

 PROJECT PRIORITIES	VISION SECTION 1	VISION SECTION 2	VISION SECTION 3
Project 1			
Project 2			
Project 3			
Project 4			
Project 5			

	WHAT WOULD YOU DO IF YOU HAD NO CONSTRAINTS?
16	
17	
18	
19	
20	
21	
22	
23	
24	
25	
26	
27	
28	
29	
30	

Take a moment to breathe

Go and make yourself a cup of tea.

The long list of dreams

Hopefully that exercise stretched you. As you got further down the list, you should have come up with things that you wouldn't normally consider. That is why it is worth taking a moment or two before you continue. Look back at your list. Which ones do you like? Are you already dismissing some because they are too difficult? Think about the original question: what would you do if you had no constraints?

Take another minute to think about the impossible ideas. Then ask yourself the question: Why not do those?

What do you have to do?

When you were talking to people from the council you may have come across some things that will challenge what you want to do. Was there anything in the diary exercise that will put a great strain on your time? Is there a big project coming up that you will have to promote but you are not enormously interested in?

 Night mayor

One mayor found themselves obliged to revamp their council's Old Folks' Christmas Party. It was costing more than it should and wasn't delivering value. They spent a lot of time turning it into a good event. It was success but it cost them time they could have used elsewhere.

Should this be a part of your vision?

Is it a part of what you want to do or just an obligation? For example, you could have "I'd want to see a cost-effective and enjoyable party for the elderly" as part of your vision. It is not the most rousing vision and you may not want to advertise the fact that you think it has been badly run for years. In which case, don't put it into your vision. Remember that your vision is for public consumption.

Opportunity knocks

You need to consider the opportunities you have. If you just concentrate on your own interests you may miss a great chance. It is time to think back to your discussion with your fellow councillors and the council's senior staff.

You should think about the opportunities they mentioned, they may fit in with what you want to do. You will need to work out which of these possibilities interested you the most. Consider the following areas.

- Big anniversaries

- Large projects

- Major changes

- Events and projects championed by the current incumbent

- Anything else that caught your attention

Did anything you found out spark some excitement? Or has an opportunity added a potential area for your vision? Can you continue with the current incumbent's plans and be successful? How can your interests serve the interests of the council? Spend some time working out which opportunities you shouldn't miss.

What are your priorities

The next exercise will assess not just what areas you are interested in but also why you are interested in them. If you can't justify your interest to yourself it seems unlikely that you will be able to interest others.

This exercise is solely about what interests you and why. Don't be tempted to think too much about how you might go about implementing these ideas. Your concern should be with what matters to you. You are going to have to reduce the number from the thirty in the previous exercise to seven.

Don't drop ideas because they are hard. A better way to reduce the number might be to build several different ideas into one. You might be interested in reaching out to the different faith communities in your area and you might want to make more of the civic service. You may be able to combine these into one potential project.

On the table below list the seven ideas that interest you most. Rate them out of ten based on how interested you are in them. Then scribble down a few reasons why they appeal to you

Hopefully that should have given you a clearer idea of what you are interested in achieving. Don't worry if it seems beyond you – you will come to

SEVEN TOP IDEAS		
IDEA	1-10	WHY DO YOU LIKE IT

planning and implementation later. For now you have worked out what areas you are interested in and, crucially, why they interest you.

How does this fit with your council's strategic aims?

Take a moment to think back to your council's strategic plan. Do these areas fit into it? Particularly look at the main headings of the plan. Which of your seven ideas fit under those headers?

Do you have what you need to do them?

Will you have the time?

Even with the best will in the world you are not going to have a lot of time. You are going to be busy. Maybe the question should be can you *make* time? At the moment you won't be able to answer this question but you can start thinking about it. Reflect on these questions for a moment.

- Can you reorganise your work schedule to give you more time?

- Can you get extra help with 'real life' demands such as cooking, cleaning or childcare?

- Could you share more events with your deputy?

- Can you automate or systemise your admin to save time?

It is worth considering these things because you aren't going to find a way to delegate your sleep. Perhaps you are beginning to figure out that it will be hard work to achieve all you want. Maybe it's about working out that you don't have time to do as much as you'd like. That is OK. You must remember that it is your vision. It isn't just about what you want to achieve but what you can achieve.

If nothing else, you should realise that you need to focus on what is most important. If you try to achieve everything you won't get anywhere.

Do you have the skills?

It is time to take another look at the skill audit you completed a couple of chapters ago. Look back at the results and ask yourself the following questions:

- Is it a true and fair reflection of who you are?

- Are you better in some areas than you gave yourself credit for?

- Have you overestimated your skills in other areas?

- Did you surprise yourself?

Once you are happy with your answers make a note of your three highest rated skills.

My top three communications skills

1. ....

2. ....

3. ....

My top three leadership skills

1. ....

2. ....

3. ....

Does this collection of skills naturally lead you in any direction? Is it just crying out for you to go one way? If not, look at it differently. Do you lack the skills needed to achieve what you want to? If you do this is not the end of the road. You have two choices: either you can develop the skills yourself or you can recruit people who have them.

This is a good time to revisit your skills development plan. Have you made any progress? Have you taken any action to start training or practicing? Revisit the plan and make any changes considering what you want to achieve.

SKILLS DEVELOPMENT PLAN

SKILL:	CURRENT LEVEL:	DESIRED LEVEL:
TRAINING		**PRACTICE**

SKILL:	CURRENT LEVEL:	DESIRED LEVEL:
TRAINING		**PRACTICE**

SKILL:	CURRENT LEVEL:	DESIRED LEVEL:
TRAINING		**PRACTICE**

Recruitment

The other strategy to plug the skills gap is to recruit people. This puts a different kind of pressure on you. You must think about who you are going to recruit, will you be able to find volunteers with time? It means you have to worry about whether the work is getting done in a timely manner and to the appropriate standard.

All of that said, recruiting a team does mean you can get closer to your aims. To get there you should consider the following questions:

- In what areas do you have a skills shortage?

- Would it be easier to recruit or learn the skills?

- Is it essential for you to have these skills to achieve what you want?

- Who do you know that might be able to help you?

- Who do you know that might be able to introduce you to someone who has the skills?

You will begin to recruit a team later. The important thing is to ensure that you haven't got any glaring holes in your plan. It is not about crushing your dreams it is about having achievable dreams.

There is still time before you need to have everything in place. You will have to work on your vision more before you are able to communicate what you intend to do to your team anyway.

Combining skills, interests and opportunities

You already know your vision. It is up there somewhere: Because you have already done the work it is just a matter of finding it. Now your job is to wrap everything up into one vision.

Think of the research that you have done as three circles. One is your skills, another is your interests and the third is your opportunities. Where these three overlap is what you should be doing. It is time to pull them all together. Although your vision seems to be a single entity it will be made up of different parts. So far you have narrowed thirty ideas down to seven. You are going to take another step and further narrow them down to five.

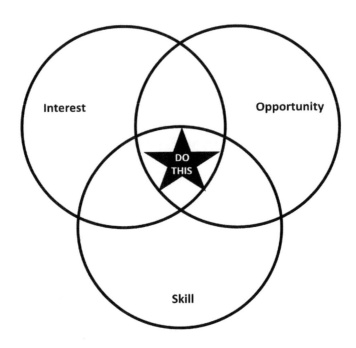

Again you may be able to merge some areas. Your idea of working with faith communities could be combined with the big community event you would like to organise. You might write 'a community cohesion project with a focus on faith groups'.

Top five areas of interest

1. ....

2. ....

3. ....

4. ....

5. ....

What are your core values?

How do you want things done?

Your vision is what you want to do. Your values are how it should be done. Obviously you have core values – you use them every day. It is time to make them explicit.

Most people have a vague idea about 'the way they want things done'. That is alright, but you are going to go further. You are going to make your vague ideas clear. That way you will always be clear about how you want to do things. Your core values will permeate everything you do.

Write down a list of things that are important to you. They might include things like punctuality, friendliness or replying to correspondence in a timely fashion. Don't worry if they initially sound silly or irrelevant. Write them down and you can look at them in more detail when you are done.

	WHAT ARE YOUR CORE VALUES?
1	
2	
3	
4	
5	
6	
7	
8	
9	
10	
11	
12	
13	
14	
15	

Now you have finished, it is time to whittle them down.

Some values you can combine. For example, if you have written 'arrive early', 'dress smartly', and 'know who you are meeting', these could be combined into 'always be properly prepared for events'. Or, better yet, 'offer exceptional service to all event organisers'.

You might choose to reject some of them for being too difficult, for example 'get on with everyone'. Or you may wish to rephrase some of them. Instead of 'getting on with everyone' you could 'do your best to engage everyone'.

Some of your initial ideas may not be that relevant. You may firmly believe in the renationalisation of the railways but it is unlikely to be at the heart of what you are going to do. Once you have had a sort-through you should end up with a few core values. Try to distil these down to three.

Core values

1. ....

2. ....

3. ....

Once you have decided on three core values it is worth taking time to consider how they will apply to what you do. Take the value, 'offer exceptional service to all event organisers'. This clearly has a lot to it and you could break it down like this.

How can you deliver exceptional service?

- Promptly decide whether you can attend an event or not

- Arrive early

- Make sure you are properly prepared and briefed

- Be friendly and courteous throughout

- Try to make people feel special

- Don't outstay your welcome

- Follow up in a timely fashion

Spend the next five minutes thinking about how you are going to live your core values. How do they apply to how you will behave while in office? How do they apply to the way you organise yourself? How do they apply to how you will treat your team?

Team values

Your core values will impact on everything your do. It could be said that they should impact on everything that is done in your name. So it is important for your team to know what your core values are.

It is not a great idea to visit your team and tell them what values they should live up to and how they should be doing their job. That never works. Instead you could do an exercise with them that is similar to the one above. Get the team together. Get them to brainstorm their core values. Then consider what it is like for someone inviting you to an event. Think about it from the initial invite, through the event, to any follow up. How do these values impact on each section of the process?

Doing this should take around two hours so it will take time out of your civic team's day. Don't demand that it is done. Try meeting with the team manager and explaining that it is something you are keen to do. They may be interested. It can be a really positive experience. As the whole team develops their core values they are all motivated to live up to them.

Back to your vision

While your core values probably won't affect what you are hoping to achieve, the time you have spent thinking about something else will have helped the thought-process. Take a minute or two to go through your areas of interest. Restate them only this time you need to whittle them down to four.

Top four areas of interest

1. ....

2. ....

3. ....

4. ....

What is your vision?

Write that vision statement

A vision statement is about the change you want to see, it is about how the world should be. It is all the impact you are going to have summed up in a few lines. The trick to writing a great vision statement is to combine everything you have thought about so far into a few words. Let me explain the process through my own vision statement.

My vision

My first interest area was meeting people. I wanted to meet lots of people. In fact, I wanted to meet everyone in my home town of Abingdon. The reason I wanted to do that was because the mayor should be visible. But, more importantly, the mayor is the best links between a council and its community. The mayor is how a council shows people that it is friendly and human.

My second area of interest was in working with young people. I got involved in politics pretty young. For me, an important part of serving my town was in showing young people that there are positive role-models both in politics and in their community. I wanted to show them that you don't have to be old to be mayor and you don't have to be old to be an active part of your community.

My time in office coincided with a major council project. We were revamping Old County Hall, which is the focal point of the town centre. I wanted to use the platform to talk about what a great facility it would be. The project was scheduled to finish after I would have left office but I wanted people to know that the disruption was worth it.

That's where I was when I'd done the exercises in this chapter. I knew I wanted to be visible, to inspire young people and to spread the word about our major project.

That is a mission not a vision

They are all things that I wanted to do but a good vision statement shows people the results of what you are going to do. It is often tempting to just talk about what you want to do because it is easier. The thing is people don't care about the work that needs to be done. What people care about is the outcome; they care about what they will get.

You need to make sure that your vision statement doesn't talk about things that need doing. You need to talk about how it will be when it is done. I shouldn't talk about meeting people, I need to talk about what results from meeting the mayor. I shouldn't talk about inspiring young people, I need to talk about what will happen to them. I shouldn't talk about communicating the council's message, I need to talk about what a community is like when it is connected to its council.

If I apply those ideas what do I end up with?

What do I want to see?

A mayor who meets everyone is part of a community that is connected and cohesive. People who have met the mayor understand a little more about how their local council works. People who have met the mayor should feel a little bit more involved in the life of their community. So I need to talk about a council that is truly connected to its community.

Young people who have been inspired by a politician are more engaged in the political process. They are more involved in their community. They are going to do more things to help their community. They may even try to get elected to the council; heck, they may even end up as mayor. So I need to talk about young people that are involved in the life of their community.

Finally, if people understand why the council is carrying out major works they will be less troubled by the disruption. If they can see how great the project will be they will be better disposed towards it. Ultimately, if they understand the council's projects they will feel better connected with the council.

All of this together will result in a town and a council that people will feel more pride for.

Short and sweet

I need to take these thoughts and make them pithy. This isn't going to happen overnight. It will take time and effort. If I look at my vision I would begin by reducing it down to something like this:

As Mayor of Abingdon I want to:

- See a council that engages the people it serves

- See young people that are a part of their community's life

- See a council that is connected to its community

If I was feeling a bit more poetic I might write it like this.

"I want to live in a town with a visible and caring local council. I want to live in a town with a vibrant community that young people want to be a part of. I want our council to be connected to its community. I want to represent a town and a council we can all be proud of."

It is simple clear and to the point. It will take you a lot of time to get your vision to sound like that. No one can just jot down a succinct vision in ten minutes. Mind you, as you have got this far through the book you clearly have vision. You can see the benefits of what you are doing rather than just concentrating on the work that needs to be done. That will help.

Back to you

Now it is your turn. Restate your areas of interest – only this time you are going to get ruthless and narrow it right down to only three.

Top three areas of interest

1. ....

2. ....

3. ....

So close you can see it

You are getting there. You have made some great progress along the road to being a twenty-first century mayor. Your vision is a big hill on that road. You aren't quite there yet but at least you can see the peak. You will keep chipping away at your vision. Yes, it will be hard work but it will come together. It will serve you throughout your time in office.

What to do now

What would you do if you could do anything?

- Do it!

What might get in the way?

- Think about all the things that could get in the way of your plans. Consider what you will need to implement your ideas and how it impacts on your vision.

What are your core values?

- Revisit them and check that you are happy with them. Consider if there is a way you can share them with your civic team.

What is your vision?

- Begin to drill down into what you want to see. This won't happen overnight but if you keep working at it then eventually you will have a clear and concise vision.

Get Organised

"If you make an effort to do your job well, your professionalism will carry you through".

Fiona Woolf, Lord Mayor of London 2013-2014

An exciting challenge

You are getting to grips with the challenge in front of you. You can see so much that you can achieve, these are exciting times. You have a right to be excited. But it is tinged with worry. It is perfectly normal to worry that you are not worthy of the office.

It is natural to be concerned that you won't live up to this great responsibility. But that worry comes from being able to see what a great opportunity it is. And you can only see that because you are preparing properly. It is the most obvious sign that you are worthy, that you are going to be a great civic leader.

You are reaching an exciting point in the journey. But that isn't because you are going to look at organisation. Managing your diary is not that exciting but it is important. It gives you a solid base to build from. It is the foundation for all the good stuff. It is important and therefore it can be daunting. You are going to have a lot of things to keep on top of. There will be many events, many people and many emails and you will have to keep track of them all.

While it is a big organisational responsibility there are massive rewards in getting it right. You can get to the point where it runs smoothly, where there is little wasted effort and no lost scraps of paper. Done right it can be your launch pad to success. Being in the right place at the right time with the right stuff is 90% of the battle.

Get Organised

What is your organisational style?

- Maybe you are a super tidy, organisational machine, maybe you are not.

How is your diary going to work?

- It is one of the most important things for your year, get it right.

Do you want to change the way things are organised?

- Maybe you want to but you must consider if it is the right thing to do.

Can you afford it?

- It can be an expensive hobby.

Do you get time off?

- You are going to be busy, but how busy is busy?

What is your organisational style?

Maybe you think you are organised, maybe you think you aren't. Somewhere between these two extremes is the truth. If you consider your organisational style you can work out if you need to pay real attention to organisation.

Read the character descriptions below then work out which one describes you best. You may find yourself drawn to more than one profile. That is OK, but if you find yourself drawn to all of them is probably worth reading them again.

The big thinker

You like to organise the whole of the project. You like to take something from the initial idea right through to delivery. You are a starter/finisher. You like the broad brushstrokes rather than the narrow details. If someone gives you a task you want to know why it needs to be done.

The practical mind

You like order, you love detail. Your desk is immaculate; everything is in its place because there is a place for everything. You have colour-coded notebooks and all your information is in the right file. You are all about how. If someone gives you a task you immediately begin to think about how to do it.

The creative one

You work on many projects at one time. You have a wide range of interests and can find yourself fascinated by a new subject. You have no difficulty thinking your way around a problem. You don't like deadlines but when they loom you kick into overdrive and get the job done. If you are given a task you will work on it if it is interesting.

The People Person

You are interested in people not things. You get excited by relationships not spreadsheets. You work well in a team but find working alone uninspiring. You would rather get on the phone than tidy your desk. If you are given a task you think about the people who have the skills to help you complete it.

Which type are you?

This is not a rigorous psychometric assessment. It is intended to help you begin to think about your organisational skills and your attitude towards ordering and managing things. It is OK to belong to two types. You could be a creative, people person or a practical big thinker. That is fine – in fact it will probably help. Here are some things to think about based on your organisational style.

The Big Thinker

It is clear that you won't have a problem with developing a strategy. Strategy is what you do well. Where you may struggle is with the frenetic nature of the role. Rather than being able to neatly start one project and work it through to completion you will have many projects on the go at once. You will have to deal with them when you can and in order of urgency. Try to pay particular attention to the fine detail of your arrangements.

The Practical Mind

You will be fine. You will thrive on the challenge of organising a large and complex diary. In fact, you will probably enjoy bringing a bit of order to it. Just try not to get bogged down in the detail. You will need to pay particularly attention to your vision. Make sure you discuss it with someone you trust who is more of a big thinker. Keep reminding yourself where you are going long-term and not just where you should be next.

The Creative Ones

You will have no shortage of ideas. The challenge for you will be in keeping focus and getting them done. Once you have a strong vision you can use your creativity to come up with novel ways of implementing it. Just keep an eye on the nitty-gritty. Have you developed techniques to help with organisation? Can you rely on your escort for help? What could your PA do to help you? You are going to find the day-to-day organisation harder than most. Give it some thought. Use your lateral thinking to come up with ways to help yourself.

The People Person

You are well suited to this job. You are going to have no problems engaging people so you will thrive at events. You will also do well at recruiting and organising a group of people to help you achieve your aims. You should use these people to help you develop your vision. They will keep you on track, as will your PA and your escort. Be careful though. Being a civic leader can be a lonely job. Often you will be on your own and relying on yourself and this is not necessarily your forte. Think about how you can excel on your own.

Everyone has organisational challenges. No-one has all of the necessary skills. The advantage you have is that you have started to think about them now. Make a few notes about your problem areas and how you can work around them.

My organisational style ....

Problem areas ....

....

....

Potential solutions ....

If you are concerned about organisation you can do three things. Firstly, you can really work on building a relationship with your secretary: if you are honest and tell them what is concerning you then they will try to help. Secondly, get yourself some training and then put in a lot of practice. Finally, you can get some extra help: work out what you need and get someone on your team who can provide it.

How is your diary going to work?

It would be unusual if you didn't keep some sort of diary. Maybe it is a traditional paper diary, a calendar in your office or kitchen or an electronic diary run through Google, Microsoft or another provider. The problem now is that your diary is not your own. A bit of your diary belongs to your secretary, a part to your deputy and it's even nice to let your family in on the deal.

As it is no longer your diary, your approach doesn't matter. In some respects, it is only important how your council organises your diary.

How do they think your diary will work?

If you have spent time as deputy mayor or council chair then you should have a good idea of how the diary works. Even if you think you know there are two good reasons to set up a meeting with your PA. Firstly, you *cannot* be too clear on this subject. You need to know rather than think you know. Secondly, you should never miss a chance to build your relationship with them.

You really do need to get on with your secretary. They hold the keys to your kingdom. They can have a massive effect on your chance to affect your community. Put bluntly they can make your life very difficult.

Fact finding mission

- How is the diary organised? Online, email or paper?

- How is event information presented to you? By email or in person?

- How often are you expected to physically meet your PA to discuss diary issues?

- What can you do to help the process run smoothly?

- Is there anything else you would like to know?

You may be tempted to tell them all about your vision and your values. It is OK to mention things if they come up naturally but don't bombard them with grand plans. You will need to tell them what your vision is but do it at the right time. If this is your first meeting concentrate on building a relationship.

The other side of the story

Hopefully you remember what the previous incumbent said about how the diary works. Did they rave about how well it was organised? Did they say it could be better? It's likely their idea of how things worked is different to that of their secretary. It is not that your secretary will deliberately mislead you, it is that they probably think it works better than it does.

Once you have worked out how the diary is organised you should give some thought to how this will fit in with the way you organise your personal diary. If you aren't careful you can end up updating things in three places. That is how things get missed.

Do you use events sheets?

Many councils use an event sheet to make sure that all the information needed for an event is provided ahead of time. Here is an example. Some are unnecessarily unwieldy but this one has about the right amount of information. It provides what you need but doesn't give the event organiser kittens.

What is important is to figure out how this information will be delivered to you and how you will make sure you have a copy to hand. Will you keep it as a PDF on your phone or do you want a physical copy? Make sure you have a strategy as nothing is worse than trying to find an address when you are about to leave for the event.

EVENT SHEET

Name of function:	
Organisation:	**Date:**
Arrival time:	**Departure Time:**
Name of contact (on the day):	**Phone number (on the day):**
Venue Address:	**Postcode:**

Number of people expected:

Ages of any children expected:

Will refreshments be provided?

Dress code:

Programme of events:

Details of any speech the mayor will be expected to make?

 Night mayor

A mayor with a young child was worried about the cost of childcare. She wasn't sure which events were appropriate to take her child to. If her council had used event sheets they could have added a question. And she could have saved a fortune.

What could you add?

If you have a special requirement, ask if the sheet can be amended. This small change can make a big difference.

Do you want to change the way things are organised?

If you are anything like me you will take one look at a system and say 'this could be done better'. If the system is ineffective then why wouldn't you want to change it? What you must remember is that civic leaders are transient, they come and go. The staff will still be working with the system next year and the year after that.

Organisational change is difficult. To do it you need the support of everyone concerned. You need them to recognise the advantages of these changes. They need to be a positive part of the process because most systems simply won't work if the people operating them do not want them to work.

Be very careful before you even think about suggesting a change to the system. Take a moment to consider the following questions.

- Do you have the time and energy needed to change it?

- Will the effort you go to changing it save you enough time to justify that investment?

- Could you spend that time accomplishing another aim?

- Did you accept this role so that you could make the council's office function smoother?

If you feel that you need to try to make a change to the way your diary is organised then you should meet with the civic manager or their equivalent and try to work on it together. This is not a book on change management but let me give you one piece of advice: *do not* make an enemy of your secretary.

Can you afford it?

Finances

You are a generous person. Mean people don't become civic leaders; they are not suited to it. Which means when someone asks you if you would like to buy some raffle tickets you will say yes. This is fine until you get asked that question ten times a week. If you can easily afford to spend £100 a week on raffle tickets then you don't need to worry too much about this section. If you have grand plans but not such grand finances it is time to do a little thinking.

Financial planning exercise

You will be given an allowance to cover your out of pocket expenses and perhaps even compensate you for a loss of potential earning. Allowances vary from the generous to the inadequate so the first thing you need to do is find out how much yours will be. Then you must find out what you have to spend it on. Sometimes your allowance is for you to spend as you chose, sometimes it will have to cover certain events.

Do you have to finance food and drink after your inauguration meeting? Are you expected to finance a Christmas party? Will you be buying drinks after the civic service? Are you planning on investing in some training? If you aren't sure give the civic team a quick call. Complete the table below to see how it will look.

Allowance   £ ....

Cost of things you have to pay for   £ ....

Actual allowance	£ ....
Deduction for tax at your current income tax rate	£ ....
Net allowance	£ ....
Monthly allowance	£ ....

Does that look like a big number? Will it last all month?

If you spend ten pounds on raffle tickets at each event how many events can you go to? How many times can you fill your car with petrol? A civic ball, for example, may well cost £100 for two tickets, £20 for a bottle of wine and £20 for raffle tickets. You can easily spend £150 in an evening. It is likely that your allowance won't cover many evenings like that. Now imagine that the tickets are £100 each, your partner needs a dress or a dinner suit and you need to get a taxi there. You could be looking at more like £500. By their very nature charity fundraisers are an expensive business.

It is easy to say 'it is only a year, don't worry'. If you can afford to do that great. If you aren't convinced, try to think a little bit about your own finances. What can you personally afford to spend on top of your civic allowance? Add that to the table below.

Monthly allowance	£ ....
How much more can you afford?	£ ....
Total monthly budget	£ ....

Does that look like it will get you through? I would ask how many raffle tickets will it buy but then you'd think I have an obsession with them. I suppose the question is: does it look like enough?

If you are concerned you could have a chat with a previous civic leader: ask them how much they think you will be spending. They may not be able or willing to give you blow-by-blow details but they should give you an idea.

If you are still worried then keep an eye on what you spend. Set yourself a realistic monthly budget; once you get close to it you will have to be more careful. It will also help if you look ahead and identify any expensive events coming up. That way you can budget for them too.

How generous should you be?

It is easy to get carried away. You are a pillar of the community. You are the mayor. You have had a glass or two of wine. And bang, you have just bought a four-foot statue of a gurning homunculus' for £250. If you find yourself in situations like this then it's best to remember the exercise you have just completed. That should sober you up quickly.

You will be invited to many charity events, including black-tie fundraisers, that promise an evening of unalloyed joy for just £100 a ticket. You do not have to go to these events. In fact, there is a compelling argument that says you *should not* go even if you can afford them. After all, these events won't further the aims of the council. These events won't further your aims. These events aren't really a good use of your time.

Your allowance and tax

You will be required to pay tax on the allowance that you receive so it is worth thinking about how you'll handle this. You don't want to be presented with a large tax bill. Tax is complex. If you have any doubts you should seek professional help. The other obligatory caveat is that all this information was correct at the time of printing.

Some of the things that you spend money on during your time in office can be offset against the tax that you will have to pay. If you spend all of your allowance on the appropriate things then you won't have to pay any tax.

It is important to note that the only items that are tax deductible are those that are purchased wholly and exclusively in pursuit of your office. In addition, you can't claim for things that your council has provided for you. So you can't claim for postage as your council will provide it.

Here are a few things that may be tax-deductible.

Travel

So long as you have not been given a chauffeur-driven car then you can claim a deduction of 45p per mile. You can also claim 20p per mile for cycling to events.

Entertainment

Entertaining expenses which are incurred wholly, exclusively and necessarily in the performance of the office holder's civic duties are deductible. So wine after council meetings is deductible, wine because it's Friday isn't.

Clothes

Unless you are purchasing something that is obviously a part of the uniform of the office then clothes are not deductible. The suit you bought to look presentable at Mayor Making is not tax deductible but you do look nice in it.

Charity

Charity donations are unlikely to be deductible. If you are planning on donating a lot you could set up a scheme that would be acceptable to the taxman.

Secretarial support

You can claim for office support if you have not been offered something similar by your council. This may in practice be quite difficult to claim.

Home office

If you are using some of your home as an office, used solely in pursuance of your duties, you can claim a contribution to overheads.

The good news is that this book is tax deductible

Books, training, or coaching that you pay for are deductible – so long as they are wholly and exclusively in pursuance of your office. Just remember to keep receipts where you can, record what you spend and set aside some money for the tax bill. This will make filing your return and paying the bill a lot easier.

If you are in any doubt you should consult a tax expert, more information can be found on HMRC's website.

Do you get time off?

Yes and no

Make the most of any time you aren't at engagements. You will be busy, so savour the time when you are not. Spend it wisely: see your family, enjoy your hobby, have a long bath, whatever relaxes you and makes you happy. I strongly suggest that you book a holiday. Where was that quiet period during the year?

That is the yes... time for the no

> **Quick Win**
>
> Check that diary and book out two weeks. Phone the office, phone work, phone your family; tell them you are going away.

The flip side is that you can take time off but you *cannot* stop being a civic leader. For the whole of your time in office you will always be a civic leader. It doesn't matter whether you are in the office, at an engagement, in the pub or even in the shower, you don't stop being a civic leader. It is literally a twenty-four hour a day job.

You do not get time off. You can be doing your shopping and someone will say hello. You'll be walking down the street and some kid will shout "it's the mayor". You don't have to sleep in your chain but you do have to behave yourself twenty-four hours a day. That really is the pressure of being a civic leader.

You are smart enough to realise this means you shouldn't do anything stupid. You shouldn't do anything you wouldn't be happy seeing on the front page of the local paper.

How is your vision statement coming along?

In the next few chapters you will concentrate on writing your vision statement. To prepare for that, look back at the three ideas you came up with at end of the last chapter. Are you happy with them? It is not too late to change. Spend a few minutes making some notes on how you might write them as a vision statement. Here is my vision statement to give you an idea of what you are aiming at.

As Mayor of Abingdon I want to:

- See a council that engages the people it serves

- See young people that are a part of their community's life

- See a council that is connected to its community

Now it is your turn.

ONLINE STRATEGY SHEET

What are you good at?		
What is being done well now?		

How much time do you have?	Per day:	Per week:
Who will help?	**What will they do?**	

What will you achieve?

- ☐ Informing
- ☐ Outreach
- ☐ Promoting

What medium will you use?

- ☐ Blog
- ☐ Video
- ☐ Facebook
- ☐ Twitter

Where will you post?

- ☐ Your website
- ☐ Council's website
- ☐ Facebook
- ☐ Twitter
- ☐ YouTube
- ☐ Other: _____

What will you post?

Don't worry if it doesn't sound like pure poetry yet. There will be plenty of opportunities to improve on it.

Heavyweight organisation

There is a lot to think about. Unless you are super organised, have the perfect PA and loads of money you are going to have to spend some time thinking about those things. Make sure you return to anything that is worrying you over the next few days.

Inspiration is the seed of achievement but organisation is where it grows.

What to do now

What is your organisational style?
- It is great if you are comfortable with the organisational challenge. If not get some help. Think about the people or technologies that could make the difference.

Find out how your diary is going to be run
- You should be totally clear on how it will work and how you can combine it with your own diary.

Build a relationship with your PA
- Meet them and get to know them. They are one of the most important people in your team.

Can you afford your time in office?
- Work out your budget and if it will be enough. Make sure you consider big items like clothing and training. Always remember how generous you can afford to be.

Have you got your tax affairs in order?
- Set up a system to record what you have spent. Set aside some money to pay your tax bill.

Have you booked that time off yet?
- If not go and do it *now*. Then you can start looking forward to that well-earned break.

Have you begun writing your vision statement?
- If not take the next five minutes and make a start.

Saying a Few Words

"The ability to cut short a speech, or extend it are useful skills. As is the wisdom to know when to do which".

Sebastian Field, Mayor of Gloucester 2015-2016

Tell them the good news

You are really beginning to get through it. You should be proud of all the exercises, meetings and mental workouts you have done. You have come along way. Of course that doesn't stop you wondering if you will be able to go the whole way. There is a lot still to do and it is OK to feel a little overwhelmed. There is much to do but you are focusing on the things that will make a difference. You could do a lot of chatting and running around and achieve very little but you are moving forward with purpose.

You are going to look at public speaking which is an essential skill for any civic leader. You will be asked to say a few words. This is great. Communicating with one person is good but having the chance to communicate with a room full of people is better. It is also nerve racking. Even if you are comfortable speaking in public, it is still hard work. It takes time to develop a good speech. It takes thought to craft an engaging message. It is hard being a good speaker. That is why most civic leaders are not very good speakers.

But you are going to be a good speaker. Because speaking well is incredibly worthwhile because it can open doors. Deliver a good speech about your vision and people will tell you how they are working toward your aims. Deliver a good speech about your event and people will seek you out to offer their help. Speaking is a precious tool in your kit.

Saying a few words.

How to get over the fear of public speaking

- Most people fear public speaking, with good reason.

How to tell people about your vision

- You can't keep your vision to yourself, it is time to get talking.

How to develop a great inauguration speech

- It is an important speech. It is never too early to start on it.

How to craft a speech for any event

- You will be making a lot of speeches, it is worth having a strategy.

How to prepare when time is short

- You should read this section if you are planning on being busy.

How to get over the fear of public speaking

You do not have to be afraid

Lots of people are afraid of speaking. That is not surprising. By speaking in public you risk failure and embarrassment in front of a room full of people you don't know. Scary stuff. Even if you consider yourself a seasoned speaker you could be in for a shock.

If you speak a lot in council meetings you might think you are a competent, confident speaker. The problem is that you are used to speaking to councillors about council business. If you go out into the world and start speaking – in places that are not council meetings, to people who are not councillors, about things which are not related to the council – you might find yourself less than comfortable. I know because that is exactly what happened to me.

You will be asked to speak in a totally different way. You will be expected to speak in a style you have never used before. Most speaking at councils is either informative or persuasive, but as a civic leader you will be expected to speak to young people. You will be expected to inspire. You will even be expected to entertain.

People get comfortable with certain situations and when they are out of those situations they get nervous. *Expect* to be nervous when you start speaking as a civic leader.

 **Night mayor**

A mayor was enjoying a community performance as part of an audience of several hundred people. That was until, without warning, the MC announced that the next person on stage would be them. It pays to always be ready to speak.

The fear cycle

If you have had a bad experience of speaking you begin a cycle which will mean that your next experience is also likely to be bad. Soon the cycle is established and you will never want to speak in public again.

If you are afraid of public speaking your body will react physically. This will manifest as tension: you will struggle to remember your words, your movements won't be natural, your mouth will dry and speaking will be harder. These physical processes will result in a poorer performance. If you find speaking hard and you don't get a good reaction you will be afraid of doing it again and the cycle will continue. It looks something like this.

The opposite is also true

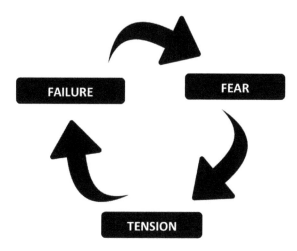

If you can begin with confidence then you will be relaxed. The reverse physical process will happen and your performance will be better. This means next time you have to make a speech you will be more relaxed and the confidence cycle will take over.

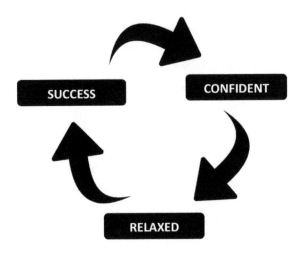

How do you begin with confidence?

Confidence comes from one of two places: experience or preparation. Experience brings confidence. You'll always have confidence when you have a lot of experience, and that means experience speaking in different places, to different audiences, on different subjects, in different styles.

But what do you do if you don't have the experience? Preparation is a great substitute. If you have prepared properly you will be confident. If you have developed a good speech and practiced it enough then you will be bursting with excitement at the prospect of delivering it.

So either you spend the time getting hours and hours of speaking experience or you make sure you are prepared. The choice is yours.

Join the club

There are hundreds of speaker's clubs across the country. They exist to help people like you to develop and hone your speaking skills. They are also great places to increase your confidence. Jump onto Google and find the nearest one. Go along for an evening to give yourself an experience of speaking in a different situation. If you have the time you could join and really improve your speaking.

How to tell people about your vision

You have already begun to develop a vision. Now it is time to start thinking about how to talk about it. True not every speech you make will feature your vision but often the event that you are speaking at will touch on your aims for the year. It is a good idea to acknowledge that and share your vision, it is not that you should make the same speech again and again it is just if you are comfortable talking about your vision you will always have something when people ask you to say a few words.

To maximise your ability to tell people what you are going to do you will develop three different ways of speaking about your vision.

- A longer speech about your complete vision

- A thirty second vision summary

- Three one to two minute speeches about your vision's sections

A longer speech about your complete vision

This will pack all your vision into around four or five minutes. It will form the basis of the other speeches and your inauguration speech as well.

A thirty second vision summary

A quick summary of your complete vision that can be dropped into speeches, interviews or conversations when you want to quickly explain your vision.

Three one to two minute speeches about your vision's sections

This will give you speech blocks that you can drop into your talks when you need to speak about a section of your vision.

Develop don't write

The mistake many people make is to write out their speech. You don't write the way you speak. If you write it out word for word it will sound more like an essay than a speech.

What you need to do is develop it by speaking. Think about what you want to say and then talk about it. Just speak out loud, then make some notes about what came out.

Then try it again and make some more notes. If you develop your speech this way it will sound more natural.

Vision not mission

Your vision is about what you want to see and how you would like the world to be. It is important to remember that your vision is not about the work that needs to be done. This is never more important than when you are speaking. You should always talk about what you want to see. Inspire them with the destination and they will be prepared to make the effort needed for the journey.

Speaking is speaking

You need to communicate your vision to people. You will do this one to one, in interviews or by making a speech. You shouldn't think of these as different things, all you are doing is talking about your vision.

Explaining your vision to one person will help prepare you for speaking about it to a large group. This is useful as there are a lot of people you will need to explain it to in a one-to-one situation. This is one of the best ways of working out how to say it so it is understood. It helps you to get familiar with saying it but also lets you judge how much impact it will have.

A longer speech about your complete vision

Sometimes you will need to talk about your vison so it is worth developing a speech that will stand on its own. To do that it will need a beginning, a middle and an end.

Introduction

Your introduction should set out what you are talking about in a sentence or two. This will briefly cover what you will say and how you can see something better for your community.

Surprising statistics or quotes make good openings. Stories make good introductions too but they need to be both short and relevant. Something startling that people are not expecting is a good way to get everyone's attention.

Don't open with a joke: if it isn't funny you have lost the audience before you have started. And don't be tempted to talk about why you have chosen what you have chosen. This will take too long and lack bite and relevance.

Main body

The main body of your speech will be made up of the sections of your vision. Each will make up a subsection of your speech. This means you already have everything you need. You should only need around three or four sentences for each section. Try to link each section of your vision together so there is a flow to your words.

Conclusion

Finally, you need to wrap it up with a conclusion. This should sum up everything you have said in a couple of sentences. It should round everything off to make your vision, and of course the speech, feel complete.

Keep at it

This is a difficult thing to do. It'll undoubtedly take some time to develop and hone your vision speech. But it will help you greatly with speaking in public as well as one to one and in the media. Take a few minutes now to get started.

If you are on your own make a few notes about each section and then try talking about them, record anything that sounds good. Don't try this if you are on the train. Make some notes and then do the talking when you get home.

It may help you to begin with the main body before writing the conclusion. Leaving the introduction to the end helps you to write an introduction to what you have actually written.

ASSEMBLING YOUR TEAM

IT GURU	SPEECH DEVELOPER
Who:	Who:
Skills:	Skills:
Tasks:	Tasks:

HOST	PR ADVISOR
Who:	Who:
Skills:	Skills:
Tasks:	Tasks:

ORGANISER	ANYTHING ELSE?
Who:	Who:
Skills:	Skills:
Tasks:	Tasks:

A thirty second vision summary

Now that you have developed a complete speech you need to spend some time trimming it down. You will need to get the whole thing down to around 30 seconds. This means you need to explain your entire theme in around four to six sentences. This may sound hard, and it will take some effort, but it will be worth it. Take it one sentence at a time.

Introduction sentence: ....

Point one sentence: ....

Point two sentence: ....

Point three sentence: ....

Conclusion sentence: ....

Try saying it out loud. What does it sound like? Don't worry if it sounds a bit clunky; you will need to keep polishing and tightening it up. The process will not only improve the words but will also help you get comfortable with saying them.

Once you can tell people about your entire vision in 30 seconds you can drop it into a speech as and when you need to. Which is great. You will also find you can drop to into conversations.

Three one to two minute speeches about your vision's sections

Sometimes you will need to expand on one section of your vision. If one of your aims is to promote community cohesion and you are at an event that is promoting unity then you will want to be able to focus on that rather than going through the whole of your vision.

To do this you should turn each section of your speech into a mini speech that lasts around one to two minutes. Just take each section of your vision speech and think about how you could introduce and conclude it. You will need to expand on what you have said but that will help you get comfortable with talking about each section.

You may also want to include a challenge at the end that motivates people into action. It is worth spending some time getting these mini speeches right. It is also worth practicing them. You will then be ready to deploy them as you need to.

Ready and willing to speak

The tasks above are not inconsiderable. But they are worth it. Once you have finished them you will have some key weapons in your arsenal.

This will give you confidence because you will never be caught with nothing to say. You will be able to drop your whole vision into a short speech, make it a part of a longer speech or drop in a section as needed. This is preparation. This will give you confidence. This will beat the fear cycle.

How to develop a great inauguration speech

Preparing for inauguration

Accepting the chains of your office is a wonderful occasion and the start of an amazing journey. It can, however, be fraught with worry and fear. For most people their inauguration speech is the biggest speech of their political career. The audience will be in the hundreds or perhaps even the thousands. This adds up to pressure.

Hopefully you are reading this with enough time to do some preparation. You would not want to get to a week before you make this big speech and realise that you haven't the faintest idea what you are going to say. Thankfully you are already most of the way there. Your speech about your vision should form the centre of your inauguration address. But there is a bit more to it than that.

What will you be talking about?

You will probably have about three minutes for your speech. That might sound like a lot but three minutes' is around 500 words. If it is more than that you are talking too fast.

Alongside your central vision you may want to advertise a forthcoming event. Don't choke your speech with plugs or it will sound like nothing more than an announcement section. Presumably what you want to advertise ties in with a part of your vision, so you should put it in your speech in the appropriate vision section.

You may also want to say thank you to a few people. This can go toward the end but don't conclude with it. Make sure you finish strongly. Don't be tempted to keep adding sections: the simpler your speech is the more people will remember what you say.

So that is the speech, then? Not exactly. It will take a lot of hard work and practice to craft and hone the best speech you can create. You should consider the following points to help you best craft your speech.

Make time

You cannot expect to develop a good speech without putting in some work. Don't leave it till the last minute. You have begun writing it and that is good. About two weeks beforehand you need to settle on what you want to say. Then you will have time to get comfortable with how you are going to say it.

The last week should be spent practicing and polishing. If you leave developing your speech till too late you will be rushing and you won't make the most of this important opportunity.

Practise

Once you have developed your speech you will need to practice it. The first few run-throughs should help you get used to what you are saying. Don't worry about anything other than getting comfortable with the words. This shouldn't take long as you have developed the speech by speaking which also helps you remember it.

Once it is firmly in your mind you will need to do a couple of run-throughs to improve your vocal variety, movement and eye contact.

Vocal variety

Monotone is boring. You need variety in your voice. Concentrate on varying the pace, power and pitch of what you say. Speaking faster can be passionate, slower can be emotional. Speaking louder can get people's attention; quieter can draw people in. Sure, you don't want to go from squeaky to gruff but if you try to put emphasis into your voice you will notice the tone changes.

The most important of all is the pause. Pause more than you think you need to and for longer than you think you should. Your pause help people understand what you are saying. It is the gaps that give the words power.

Movement

You may choose to deliver the speech from behind a lectern, which is fine. If you have the chance, however, you can add interest by moving across the stage. As you progress through your vision you could move across the stage to create an area for each section. You can move from an area where you talk about the past to another where you talk about the future.

Your hand gestures are important too. Wide open arms embrace the audience. Pointing down makes you seem grounded. Banging one hand onto the other seems passionate.

The key thing to remember is that if you move – be it with your whole body or just your hands – it should be to convey something. Random or repetitive movement makes you appear nervous. Movement with purpose makes you seem, well, purposeful.

Eye contact

Eye contact is essential to make a connection with the audience. Often inexperienced speakers scan over the top of the audience's heads. This is not eye contact. You should make clear and sustained eye contact with individuals in the audience.

Once more for a friend

Once you are comfortable with everything try performing it for a friend. It is different performing for people, even if there is only one. There is a strong chance that they will say it is brilliant. That is great but you want something more. Here are some questions designed to help them offer you some definite feedback.

- What did you like about the speech? Please be specific.

- Did the delivery seem natural?

- Was there anything that was distracting?

- What do you remember of what was said?

- Was there anything that you didn't understand?

If you can find someone that can offer you great feedback you should definitely make them a part of your team.

How to craft a speech for any event

Thank you, well done, thank you

To make a good speech you need a good structure. When I was mayor I quickly fell into a routine with my speeches. I always made the same speech. It was, basically, thank you for a great evening, well done on all the good work you're doing, thank you for the contribution you make to the community. Or thank you, well done, thank you. It is simple to remember and it works.

Thank you

It is important to stress that this does not mean open with 'thanks for inviting me', or 'thanks for letting me speak'. Both of these are easy starts but they aren't very good. They are all about you. If you start by thanking them for the invite the natural continuation is to tell them why you are so pleased to be here. The thing is that people don't care that you are pleased to be there.

If you thank them for a great evening then you are talking about them. Now the natural continuation is to tell them why the evening was great and the focus will stay on them, rather than you.

Well done

If you have been talking about what has gone well on the night you can lead straight into what the organisation is doing well. Make sure that you focus the language on them. Instead of saying that you think they are doing this well, make sure you concentrate on saying that they are brilliant.

You may want to congratulate them if they are doing something that contributes to your vision. Remember to keep it about them but don't miss this opportunity to drop in some of your prepared vision speech.

Thank you

As you have been talking about the great work they are doing it will be easy to move on to thanking them for what they have done. Talk about the positive impact they are having on the community. Just don't be tempted to make this section too long. Remember it should be a quick thank you to tie it all up.

Event exercise

As you know, the key to beating nerves is preparation. If you get a chance to practice making this kind of speech before you take office you will be more confident about making them later.

But no one asks you to speak before you take office

That doesn't mean you can't prepare. Next time you are at a community event, a fete, a concert or a celebration for a local organisation, think about what sort of speech you would make.

Use the 'thank you, well done, thank you' method. Make some notes for each section. Try delivering the speech when you get home or in the car on the way back. If you can do this a few times you will quickly get into the swing of it.

How to prepare when time is short

Worry about what you want to say, not how you are going to say it

Too many people get hung up on saying something in a very precise way. The secret to learning speeches quickly is to learn the sentiment not the words.

If you know the emotional and intellectual basis of what you are saying the words will come.

Make shorter notes

As you aren't trying to remember an exact script you do not need exact notes. All you need is a few words to jog your memory. As you are trying to catch the sentiment rather than the words you only need short notes.

Use business cards

If you only have a few keywords as notes you can fit them on the back of a business card. They can be hidden in the palm of your hand. This makes you look great as people think you have no notes. You can use bigger index-sized cards if you need more space – just do not use a scrappy old bit of A4.

It is just a few words

Speaking is a much-underrated skill among local politicians. Remember that it doesn't feel like a long speech when you are giving it but it often does when you have to listen to it. If you try to be yourself and practice hard you won't go too far wrong.

What to do now

Are you afraid of public speaking?

- Get into a positive cycle. Try a speaker's club.

Practice speaking about your vision

- Begin by developing the longer version of your vision speech.

Prepare the thirty second speech

- Refine what you have prepared and make it compact.

Prepare the section speeches

- Develop individual speeches for each section of your vision. Make sure they are complete speeches.

Begin thinking about your inauguration speech

- It is never too early to begin preparing. A really well developed vision speech means you are halfway there.

Practice developing a speech at the next community event

- Next time you are at an event think about how you would use the 'thank you, well done, thank you' structure. It may feel stupid but practice it out loud.

RECRUITMENT

Building Your Team

"The role has been challenging but people's assistance and wisdom have been invaluable".

Tanmanjeet Singh Dhesi, Mayor of Gravesham 2011-2012

No mayor is an island

You should be proud of the amount of time you have put in to get to this point. You have easily spent more time preparing than most civic leaders ever do. You may hesitate to pat yourself on the back too quickly because you are wondering if you can find the time to finish everything that you need to. You may wonder if there are enough hours between now and when you take office. That is natural but remember you have invested your time wisely and you are getting ever closer to your goal.

Having a team will also bring you closer to your aims. It is worthwhile recruiting some help because it allows you to achieve more. Obviously, if there are many people working on a project then more work will get done. You could use some hands to lighten the load. While there are benefits there are also challenges, to start with where are you going to get these people from? And once you have recruited them you need to ensure they work to a standard and even make demands of them. Leading a team is tough.

But despite the hardship there are real rewards to be had. Any project of any value is the result of collaboration. Because working together improves the quality. Your team will have ideas that you would never have thought of. They will know techniques that will save time and money as well as improving the standard. Yes, your team will help you do more but it is not just the quantity that counts, your team will deliver bundles of quality too.

Building Your Team

Are you a leader?

- Are you ready to become a civic leader?

What do escorts do?
- Take a look at the most important member of your team.

What will your team look like?
- Where do you need help and who is going to provide it?

How do you recruit people?
- The all-important task of getting people to join the team.

Are you a leader?

There is a reason why you are called a civic leader. It is because you are going to take on a leadership role.

You will need to run the team that is going to meet your goals. You must make sure that they complete the work you have asked of them. Even more importantly, you must make sure that it is done to the standard you have set. You are the leader; it is your reputation that is on the line. If it doesn't meet the standards it is you that suffers.

Maintaining these standards can be difficult. Often you are dealing with people who are working on a voluntary basis. Of course a motivated volunteer will always work better than a bored staff member but sometimes it is hard for people to find the time to do everything they would like to.

It is tricky when you are dealing with the council's staff. Don't mistake them – most council employees are hard-working and want to do the best job they can. It is just you are not their line manager.

Leadership

Civic leaders exist in a strange hinterland. Their secretaries are obviously there to serve them yet the mayor has no real power to compel them to do anything. If you aren't recognised in the council's hierarchy then you must create your own authority.

Being a civic leader is a true test of your leadership skills. You may not consider yourself a natural leader or you may not have spent a lot of time in similar roles. But this experience is going to teach you a great deal.

This is not a book about leadership. If you feel that you need more help or training to prepare you for this then you should try to take part in a leadership training program. This may be available through your council, your employer or a training organisation such as Toastmasters International. You could also look to find a mentor either through your political party, your work or even an experienced friend that you respect.

Look back over the leadership section of the skills audit: where do your strengths lie? Where could you be better? Think about how you can use your strengths and compensate for your weaknesses. Teams need leaders. If you want a team to help then you will have to lead them.

What do escorts do?

Partner, companion, advisor

Escorts have many names and many roles. A hundred or so years ago it was simple: there were mayors and mayoresses and everyone knew which one was which. But in 1907 the Qualification of Women act gave women the right to become the first citizen. The first was Elizabeth Garrett Anderson, Mayor of Aldeburgh. Sadly, her husband died a few years before she took office but I still like to think of a perplexed town clerk wondering whether they could call him the mayoress.

And thus many, varied, and on the whole awful, new names where born, all of which tend to conjure up entirely the wrong image. Here is the official answer to who is what:

- Mayoress: The wife or female partner of a mayor

- Consort: The husband of the mayor

- Escort: A relative or friend of the mayor

- Partner: The male partner of a mayor

I'll use the phrase 'escort' because that is what is used in Abingdon. And you should use whatever phrase your council uses. It is not worth arguing about.

The first thing you have to work out is who your escort is going to be. I have never come across someone who refused to select an escort, civic leaders have them even if they don't do much and they are just symbolic.

For many it will be their life partner. But widows are often elected to the office and we live in a different world to the days of mayors and mayoresses. Some people don't have partners. There are also many cases where a councillor's significant other has been unwilling or unable to fulfil the role.

If you are unsure about who you will ask to be your escort, read what follows. It is pretty much a job description so it may help you think about who to ask.

There are really two aspects to the job: the public face and the private supporter. The public face is the person that accompanies you to events. The private supporter is the person who act as your friend, confidante and sounding board. If you are lucky these two roles will be combined in one person.

So what does an escort actually do?

There is one big misconception with escorts. Many people worry that they will have to attend every event. Don't: your escort is not expected to accompany you to everything you do. They can, if they want to, but they are not expected to. It is worth labouring this point. If you go to visit a school to open a new library the staff there really won't expect your escort to come too. If it interests your escort then they can – no one is going to complain – but they are not expected.

Sometimes it is particularly worth their attending, especially if the catering will be good. But even when you know the food will be amazing it is not essential. If you have a ticket and your escort is busy or not interested you could take a friend or family member. It is a matter of logistics and judgement whether you take your escort, someone else or no one.

When you discuss the job with your potential escort it is important to stress this. Chances are they will think they will be as busy as you are. This is not the case.

Friend, confidante, number one advisor

Every civic leader has problems. So will you. You will need someone to discuss them with. Someone that loves and understands you, takes your side, never judges you and most of all never complains. I sincerely hope you have someone like that because above every other element of your team you will need a sounding board and a dumping ground.

A good long chat

You need to talk to your partner. You need to talk to them irrespective of whether they will be your escort. Civic office can put an enormous strain on your relationship. This kind of conversation can be hard work but it is better to get everything straight before you start. The alternative is to have a conversation about who's doing the washing up when you've just returned from three events. Another word for that kind of conversation is an argument.

Being clear to start with will take some time. Don't scrimp on this. Give it the time it needs, the time it deserves. You might need to have two or three goes at it. Your relationship is more important than this job. You won't hear me say that about many things, but your relationship should come first. Your partner will be with you for life and this job is just for a year.

Points to discuss, or at least consider discussing

- What concerns do they have about the year?

- How busy do they expect you to be?

- How busy do they expect to be?

- What family events or activities do they not want you to miss?

- How do you plan to work out cooking, shopping and cleaning?

- Do you need to make any new arrangements for childcare?

- Do they have time to help with organising civic events?

- Do they have any other concerns?

You want your home life to be as smooth as possible. The life of a civic leader doesn't run entirely smoothly – but if you can get a solid base you have given yourself a good start. More than at any other time you need a warm, friendly refuge to comfort you after a hard day.

Make sure that you listen to and address your partner's concerns. Most important, remember they will be helping you a lot so make it as easy for them as you can.

A member of the team

Your partner is potentially one of the most important members of your team. Soon you will look at the composition of that team but it is worth bearing in mind that your escort can be an important member.

They may not be able to. They may only have time to accompany you to a few events. They may have a demanding job or need to concentrate on childcare and domestic responsibilities while you are busy. They may be too busy to do anything. They can, however, still act as an advisor. They will have enough skills and experience to offer you some solid advice in one or more of the areas you will be working in.

 Twenty-first century mayor

Nicholas Woolf, consort to Fiona Woolf, Lord Mayor of London, took on a section of her vision. He championed the Lord Mayor's Charity Leadership programme by hosting events and acting as an ambassador.

Take on a section of your vision

Could your escort take ownership of one section of your vision? Could they implement it for you? Could you change your vision to converge with one of their passions? This a great way for your escort to help you. They may be too busy to commit to something like this, though, and remember it is not a mandatory part of the job.

The partner's skills audit

All dire warnings about ill-feeling and domestic strife aside, your partner will be keen to help. Once you have decided on some parameters for the year it is a good idea to assess how best they can assist.

Maybe they have been clear that they don't have the time or inclination. Even so, it is worth getting them to complete the exercise. They may be able to act as a consultant. Maybe they are looking forward to helping and have already got some sort of idea of how they can best support you. It is still worth them going through this exercise as it may give them some new ideas.

It is much better for them to do this exercise. You know them well but you will get better results if they answer the questions.

	SEVEN TOP IDEAS	
IDEA	1-10	WHY DO YOU LIKE IT

EVENT SHEET

Name of function:	

Organisation:	Date:

Arrival time:	Departure Time:

Name of contact (on the day):	Phone number (on the day):

Venue Address:	Postcode:

Number of people expected:

Ages of any children expected:

Will refreshments be provided?

Dress code:

Programme of events:

Details of any speech the mayor will be expected to make?

Interpreting the results

Obviously, this isn't an exact measure of their skills but it should give you some idea of where their strengths are. If they answer yes to more questions than they answer no, they can probably be of some help. If they are putting yes to every question in a section then that is where they should help. Ultimately, it is just a way of getting you to think. If you feel that one area is most appropriate but the exercise disagrees, ignore the exercise and go with what you know.

It is not a bad idea to compare their skills with your skills. If there's an area that they are strong in and you are weak, then this could be the right place for them to help. Of course, the amount of time they have got will also affect how they can help. The table below should give you some idea of what they can do.

HOW TO USE YOUR PARTNER			
SKILL	LOTS OF TIME	SOME TIME	LITTLE TIME
Interpersonal Skills	help at events	give advice and support	be there when they can
Engaging Online	devise and implement a strategy	run social media or website	help develop a strategy
Hosting Events	run events	help at events	offer advice
Speech Development	help develop and practice speeches	help practice	listen to the final run-through
Organisation	help manage your diary and admin	meet weekly to go through diary	help develop a system
Community	run community program	run an event	devise strategy
Media	act as PR agent	help prepare for interviews	provide guidance

Make sure you don't overload them or expect too much. It is better for them to do one thing well than to struggle to do many things. Again, it is about having the conversation so that you are both comfortable with the situation.

What will your team look like?

Isn't the civic team my team?

Your civic team will do a lot for you. They will try to help as best they can. But as budgets become tighter they will find it hard to maintain even their current level of support. The bottom line is that if they can't supply something you need you should find it yourself.

That is why it is important to find out exactly what your civic team will do for you. It is vital to know who does what to make sure there are no duplications or misunderstandings.

Building the team

In an ideal world you would have nothing to do. Everything you want to achieve would be delegated. All you would have to do is sparkle. If each area of your vision had someone responsible for it you could concentrate on what you do best – sparkling.

That is unlikely. You may be able to get your escort to take charge of part of your vision. You may get your charity committee chair to take responsibility for worthy causes. The rest will be your responsibility. You will have to organise, manage and sparkle. That is the leadership bit of civic leadership.

Your team is more likely to help you out with specific problems rather than areas of your vision. It is easy to recruit someone to help you online. Could you find someone to help you engage young people?

Where will these people come from?

You know many people. All of them have skills, most of them will be keen to help you and some will even have the time to do it. You already know all the members of your team. You just have to get them to agree.

Your first port of call should be to your friends. They are the most invested in your success. Sure, they aren't going to just drop everything for the year, but they will be happy to help if they can. This isn't the only group of people you know. You also know people through your work and through your community. These people won't be as keen to help but if they buy into your vision they will consider helping.

Finally there are councillors. They may well want to help but they are busy people. Don't expect them to be falling over themselves to assist. If they have skills you need there are two things you can do.

You can ask them to act as a consultant. Most councillors would be flattered to offer you a few hours of their expertise. The other strategy is to ask them to do something specific and time-limited, like taking charge of one area of an event on the day. That would involve some thinking but mostly just turning up for an afternoon or evening. Just consider how much else they do before you ask them for something big.

Should you pay people?

There is no ideological reason for not hiring someone. If you are considering taking unpaid leave from your day job to complete a specific task it might be better to pay someone and keep working. Some tasks can be carried out by someone paid a lot less than you. Sometimes you get more done if you earn the money and pay people to do stuff.

The great thing about the internet is you can now employ people for a specific task without meeting them or even living in the same country. There are myriad websites out there like Fiverr or Upwork. If you chose to engage someone this way make sure you've done your research, give them a clear brief and treat them fairly.

What roles do you need?

Here are some ideas of positions you might consider recruiting.

Host

We all have that friend who organises awesome parties. Have you thought about asking them to help? They might be willing to take over the organisation of your Christmas party or the other social events you have to host. They might only be able to give you some tips or they may prefer to organise the behind-the-scenes stuff, leaving you out front to shine.

Speech developer

This is not a speechwriter. A skilled speechwriter will produce a speech that mirrors the way you speak. Unless you happen to know such a person you are better of getting someone to help you develop your speech.

This might seem like a luxury but it is worth considering, if only for important speeches. You can't get too much help in those situations. They should help you plan and structure the speech. Then they should help you practice it. Ideally they would give you feedback borne of experience. They should be able to give you some concrete tips on how you can improve your presentation as well as tell you what you did well.

PR adviser

Whether you want to go the whole hog and have a dedicated person to liaise with the media or not will depend on what you want to achieve. If you will be using the press a lot you should consider it. If you have the same person always dealing with the various outlets they will build key relationships.

They can also help you prepare for big interviews. They can ask you searching questions and provide quality feedback, like your speech developer. In fact the same person could prepare you for speeches and interviews.

Organisation

It is likely that your PA will be the person who helps you with organisation. It is OK to say you need extra help. Do you know someone who can assist you developing a system to help you keep on top of your diary? Even someone who could call you once a week to discuss what is coming up could help.

IT guru

You might not need help if you are an internet rock star. Otherwise, you should seriously consider getting help. You may benefit from a hand with web strategy. Your IT guru may be able to show you a few easy things you can do online. It is amazing what you can achieve with some simple tools. Or they may take an active role by doing the work. Either way you can achieve a great deal online if you have a good strategy and put in the effort.

 **Twenty-first century mayor**

Bob Smytherman, Mayor of Worthing recruited a local photographer to be his official snapper. This really helped him stand out on social media. He also has great photos to remember the year by.

Board of directors

This exercise is about thinking who you want around your boardroom table. You might not choose to fill all the seats. That is OK. If you think you need someone to fulfil a role but don't know who then leave it blank. You don't have to work out your entire team today. It is an ongoing process. It is OK if the exercise only helps you think about the skills your team needs.

If you have names for positions that is great. It is still worth taking the time to make a note of the skills you need and what work you are expecting each person to do. Ultimately it will help you develop an idea of what they can do for you.

ASSEMBLING YOUR TEAM	
IT GURU	**SPEECH DEVELOPER**
Who:	Who:
Skills:	Skills:
Tasks:	Tasks:
HOST	**PR ADVISOR**
Who:	Who:
Skills:	Skills:
Tasks:	Tasks:
ORGANISER	**ANYTHING ELSE?**
Who:	Who:
Skills:	Skills:
Tasks:	Tasks:

How do the staff fit in?

Spend some time thinking about how your civic team and your personal team will work together. It is important that they don't duplicate work. Even more importantly they shouldn't feel like there is someone else encroaching on their territory.

How do you recruit people?

Winning commitment

People like helping people. They particularly like helping people who hold offices like yours. That is good for you. First and foremost you need to talk to potential recruits. You need to communicate your vision and your passion. You need to show them that the task energises you and that this energy is infectious.

Give them the broad brushstrokes of what you are trying to do. Be careful not to outline everything in too much detail, partly because it will dilute your vision and partly because it will make them think it has all been decided. People like to be creative and to feel involved. If you tell them everything you are going to do then where is the room for their contribution?

You need to be clear on the amount of time and effort you need from them. To fulfil some of these roles is a big commitment. If you are in office for a year they could be working on the project for 18 months. Make sure that they are happy signing up to this. You will need to use all your skills of engagement, inspiration and leadership to bring them on board. And you may want to point out that they will have a fantastic new project to talk about on their CV; you could even offer them a reference.

Do you need to have team meetings?

You are assembling a team in a metaphorical sense, not necessarily physically. You probably don't need to have a big meeting. Your team may all be working on different sections of a large vision with little crossover. Don't have one because you think you should; only organise a meeting if you have a clear aim in mind. If you really want to get everyone together arrange a social event.

Be generous with your thanks

It is not unusual for civic leaders to hand out several bunches of flowers and bottles of wine at the end of their time in office. This is great but thanks are not just for the end of the year. It never hurts to offer people a small gift to remind them that you are grateful.

It is important to remember that these people are giving you their skills and their time. Don't forget how important that is. Thank them regularly. The true measure of a successful civic leader is the number of people they thank.

Reflect on what you have learnt

You could try to recruit a team of dozens of people to meet your every need but is that the support you require? Consider what you really need and put people in place to provide that. With the right people in the right places you will achieve much more.

What to do now

Do you need to work on your leadership skills?

- Make sure you are comfortable with your leadership skills. Get training or practice if you need it.

Is your partner happy?

- I cannot overstate the importance of this. You need to get everything straight with them. It will not ensure that your year is smooth but it will be a big help.

Have you got an idea of what your team will look like?

- Identify the areas you particularly need help with. Then identify people to fill those holes.

Are you clear how the staff will fit into your plans?

- Make sure everyone is clear about what they are working on. Take seriously people's feeling that their role is being encroached.

Time to Shine Online

"I want to bring the role into the modern day… Let's get the Lord Mayor on Twitter".

Carl Austin-Behan, Lord Mayor of Manchester 2016-2017

Turn excitement into engagement

You can see off in the distance the point you need to be at. You have travelled so far towards it, which is great. But then you start to wonder if you are ever going to get there. You might be thinking that you don't have the time or the energy to travel the last bit. It Is OK to feel like that. Just remember, the time that you have invested now will pay dividends. Because you are clear in what you are going to achieve you won't waste time wondering if something is right for you, because you will know.

You are now going to dive into the world of social media and online engagement. This is exciting as it gives you opportunities to engage people that weren't available to civic leaders even 10 years ago, the chance to engage many, many people. While it is a great opportunity it isn't always clear how to make the most of it. You are probably a bit overwhelmed by the variety of things you could do online. Even the range of buzz words is intimidating. Even if you can get through all that, there is no guarantee that you will see any results at all.

Yet it is worth taking a risk and plunging into the jargon infested waters. The internet allows you to keep engaging people long after you meet them. If you do it right you can get them talking before you have even seen them. You can walk through the door and people will think that they already know you. This is fantastic because it helps you to achieve what you need to. It helps you turn your vision into a reality.

Time to shine online

How much time do you have available to spend online?

- Consider how long you have to crack the internet.

How do you find your audience online?

- There are lots of people on the web, how do you find the right ones?

What are your online skills?

- You have more skills than you think.

What do you want to achieve?

- Having lots of followers isn't the best aim, what do you want to do with them?

What is the current incumbent doing?

- It will be somewhere between YouTube sensation and techno dinosaur.

What is your strategy?

- Time to get clear about what you are going to do.

How does social media fit into your vison?

- It must dovetail with all your other aims.

How much time do you have available to spend online?

Your initial reaction maybe "I don't have any time! I barely have time to do all the other things that need doing!" But you won't need a huge commitment. You can make an impact on social media with just 10 minutes a day. If you have a smartphone then you can Tweet or post on Facebook whenever you have a minute. Your ten minutes should be enough for two posts. Add a photo and mention the organisers of the event and you have done some great work, all in ten minutes.

If you want to produce something a bit longer than a Tweet then you might want to publish a blog or produce videos. An hour should be enough to write 400 words or make a 5-minute video. Then you could spend another hour putting it on your website and scheduling daily social media promotion. A great weekly update can be produced and promoted in just two hours.

If you think you might be pushed for time you could always get some help, but never get someone to pretend to be you on social media. You are the one people want to interact with, so don't disappoint them by faking it.

You may be able to get someone who can help you with the promotion. They could do the leg-work of posting and scheduling your updates. They might even be able to set up your website so that it automatically promotes your posts. One of the best things about experts is they know how you can get the most out of your time. If you know anyone who is good at web design or social media have a chat with them and listen to their advice.

How do you find your audience online?

You know what social media is. You probably have accounts on a couple of sites already. In fact, you probably use social networks daily. But, just for clarity, it is a digital space for people to get together and share things. The things they share differ, from photos of a night out to articles about China's influence on the British economy. It is all about people connecting and sharing.

What you may not have considered is just how pervasive social media is. Take a blog: in one sense it is a website that is regularly updated with articles on a subject. But the best blogs are communities. The people who read them make comments and it becomes more like a discussion than an article. Done well it becomes a digital space for people to get together and share things. Even YouTube is a community. People share videos. People comment on those videos and link to others. People get together to exchange ideas.

The internet is about connecting and sharing. And that is what makes it so powerful. If you are prepared to contribute, people will connect with you. If you are prepared to start a conversation, people will build real relationships with you.

The most important thing to remember is that you aren't there just to broadcast. You will have the most impact if you don't just pump out a message. If you share and interact then you can build genuine relationships.

Who is your audience online?

You could spend a lot of time and effort worrying about your target audience. Don't. You're interested in local people. You could spend a lot of time and effort worrying about where to find them. Don't. They're on social media.

All the big social media platforms have a lot of people on them, many of whom will be local to you. You are only in office for a short period. In that time you simply won't be able to exhaust the potential of any social media platform. All this boils down to one essential fact: social media has more potential than you have time.

You definitely won't exhaust Facebook, Twitter or YouTube. You won't exhaust the potential of a blog. You won't even get to close to finding and connecting with everyone on platforms like Pinterest or Instagram.

In technical terms, platforms are scalable. In simple terms, the potential is greater that you can exploit. So there's your market research done.

Go where you do your best work

Every social media platform has an audience so you should concentrate on the one you're most comfortable with. The one you use most. The one you enjoy most. The one where you do your best work.

If you write a great blog don't think about setting up a Facebook group. If you are some sort of Instagram ninja don't think about conquering LinkedIn. Stick to what you are good at. You may not think you have any internet skills. You may not even know what Instagram is. But even if you don't have the knowledge or experience you do have skills. They are the same skills you use offline.

You just need a strategy. You are going to work out what you are good at and what is being done already. Then you will figure out what you are going to do. That is all an online strategy is: what you are good at, what you have got, what you are going to do. Simple.

What are your online skills?

Online skills audit

Think back to the skills audit. How did you rate for engaging online? Have another look at those skills and think about what you might want to do online. Then answer the questions below and read the descriptions and you will know where to best deploy your skills. There are four main options

HOW TO USE YOUR PARTNER

SKILL	LOTS OF TIME	SOME TIME	LITTLE TIME
Interpersonal Skills	help at events	give advice and support	be there when they can
Engaging Online	devise and implement a strategy	run social media or website	help develop a strategy
Hosting Events	run events	help at events	offer advice

for engaging people online. You can start a blog, produce videos or you can use Facebook or Twitter. You don't have to just stick to one of these – in fact you should combine them to achieve the best results.

Writing a blog

You are comfortable writing article at around 400 words or more. You think you could write a paragraph on each event and string them together into a weekly catch-up of what you have been doing. You are good at writing engaging headlines. If this describes you then you are probably best suited to starting a blog. If you can take good photos they will help too.

Producing videos

You are comfortable on camera and reasonably technical. In which case you should work with video. You could produce a video diary, in the form of a weekly catch up of where you have been.

Facebook

You would rather be friendly than formal. You are happy responding to people's comments. You can write short punchy sentences. You are good at taking photos. Then you will do your best work on Facebook.

Twitter

You are comfortable using mobile apps. You can write short punchy sentences and catchy headlines. You are good at taking photos. It doesn't matter if you want to be informal or not. If this is you then Twitter is probably the best platform.

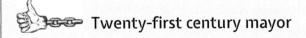 **Twenty-first century mayor**

Mark Harris, Mayor of Cirencester, has built a following on Twitter by regularly sharing information that is of interest to local people. They follow him so that they can find out what is going on in their community, and whilst they are there they also see what he is promoting. You can find him @MrMarkHarris.

But you like LinkedIn

LinkedIn is a business network. There are well over 15 million registered users in the UK. They haven't signed up to see videos of sneezing pandas. They are there to do business.

So can you do business with them? Of course. One of the handiest ways to keeping in touch with professional people is through LinkedIn. Think of it as a giant online contact book. But don't make it your focus. It isn't particularly good for advertising events. In fact, some people would take a dim view of it because that isn't what LinkedIn is for. Use it but don't make it your mainstay.

Personal or professional?

There is always a tension with presenting yourself. Do you present the image that you think people expect of the office or should you just be yourself? This tension exists just as much online. Is it OK to share personal stuff on your mayoral account or should you remain professional at all times? The simple answer is that you must balance these two parts of yourself.

There are parts of your life that it is probably best to steer clear of, I won't judge you if you enjoy nudist bungee jumping but some might. Then there are parts of your life that you may not wish to use for promotional purposes, like your family. But it is alright to share a bit of personal detail. If you just made an amazing cake show us the photos. Wish your friends happy birthday. Recommend a good film. Don't go crazy but you aren't a robot, people appreciate it if you show them your human from time to time.

What do you want to achieve?

In the real world plans that lack direction are just meaningless lists. The same is true online: engagement isn't an end in itself. Just meeting people and making yourself popular serves little purpose. To really get to grips with what you need to do online you need to know what you want to achieve.

Outreach

You will meet a wide range of people during your time in office, but it is certain that there are groups that you will meet more than others. As every demographic is interacting online you could reach any specific groups of people you need to. Which groups do you want to connect with?

Promotion

There are bound to be people who would love to support your events but just don't know they are happening. Maybe the internet could help. You could also use it to promote your vision.

Informing

People are interested in what goes on in their community. If you tell people you are visiting a school fete you may not advance your vision but you are offering useful information. Don't underestimate how powerful this can be. Most people would like to know more about where they live.

What could you achieve?

Becoming an internet rock star is a long hard road. If you expect to put yourself online and instantly be swamped by adoring fans you will be disappointing. With hard work and dedication you could increase your followers in a year by between a few hundred and a few thousand. The secret to doing that is:

- Be present

- Be consistent

- Interact with people

Stick at it and make sure you say hello to me, I'd love to follow you.

What is the current incumbent doing?

You need to consider what already exists. What is the ground that you are building on? If there is nothing then you have a clean slate and, in some ways, that is better. You won't feel obliged to carry something on. If the current mayor is rocking it all over the web then it will be easy. Just keep up the great engagement they have been doing. The chances are that it will be somewhere in between.

Fact-finding mission

It is worth having a chat with the current incumbent to find out not just what they are doing but what is going well.

- Does the website stand alone or is it part of the council's?

- Do they use Twitter?

- Is there a Facebook page?

- Do they have a blog?

- Do they have a YouTube page?

- What is working best?

- Is there anything else you would like to know?

It is not about the website

It is always nice to have a great website but it is not essential. Many people have made a great impact on the internet with a blog on Medium, videos on YouTube or photos on Instagram. They didn't need websites. They achieved what they wanted to using other platforms.

There are advantages to having your own website. If it is your site, you are in control. Facebook is notorious for changing the rules. Over the years, they have made it harder for people to discover you unless you pay for advertising. If you rely on Facebook you could see your hard work spoiled because they have decided to make a change. You can also use your site to sell tickets for events. But then again you could direct people from your social media page to a ticket-sales platform like Eventbrite.

So if you don't have a website or it isn't very good and you can't change it – don't despair. It is better to have your own web presence but you no longer need a website to be great on the web.

> ### Quick Win
>
> Type the name of your office into Google and see what happens. Then repeat the process with YouTube, Facebook and Twitter.

 Twenty-first century mayor

If you want to know what a great mayoral website looks like visit www.mayor.cityofwolverhamptoncouncil.co.uk/ or pop 'Mayor of Wolverhampton' into Google. They have done a great job of remaining true to the history of the office but also looking thoroughly twenty-first century.

How will you promote your posts?

The internet is full of great content that nobody ever sees. If you choose to write a blog or publish videos on your site you need a way to tell people what you are doing. You can, of course, do this in person. You can put your web address and social media contacts on your business cards. You can drop it into your speeches, "as I said recently on my blog".

Another great way of promoting your work is to use social media. Try putting out some attention-grabbing Tweets or Facebook updates with a link to your blog. These work particularly well if you use an eye-catching image too. If you are consistent with your promotion then you will start to build a following. Most blogging platforms have a way of automatically promoting your posts on social media. This can really save you time. If you don't know how to do this ask an internet savvy friend.

You need to be a bit careful about how often you promote your stuff. You need to Tweet something more than once before most people will notice. If you are doing a weekly blog-post or video you could easily tweet about it twice a day every day that week. But don't do that on Facebook or LinkedIn: people are less tolerant of seeing the same thing again and again so just share it once on those sites.

Of course, if you are just planning on publishing your stuff on a social media site then you will need to handle the promotion differently. You should still share some links on other social media to make sure as many people know as possible, but don't overdo it on the main site. Some people get put off if they see you promoting you posts too much.

What is your strategy?

Forming a plan

This need not be as complicated as it sounds. You have already answered the main questions. You have got what you need to fill out the social media strategy form:

ONLINE STRATEGY SHEET

What are you good at?

What is being done well now?

How much time do you have?	Per day:	Per week:

Who will help? | **What will they do?**

What will you achieve?

- [ ] Informing
- [ ] Outreach
- [ ] Promoting

What medium will you use?

- [ ] Blog
- [ ] Video
- [ ] Facebook
- [ ] Twitter

Where will you post?

- [ ] Your website
- [ ] Council's website
- [ ] Facebook
- [ ] Twitter
- [ ] YouTube
- [ ] Other: _____

What will you post?

How will you tell people what you are doing?

What do you need to do before you take office?

You may wonder what you are going to post. You will be posting about engagements or events that you are promoting. You can do this either daily or as a weekly roundup. This could mean tweeting about engagements at least once a day, sharing a photo on Facebook every other day or writing a blog post once a week. It doesn't have to be complicated.

Whatever you plan to do it is important to develop a strategy. If you are clear before you start it will make it easier for you to be consistent – and consistency is very important. People will follow you if you post things regularly; if you are hit-and-miss they won't bother to check for updates.

How does social media fit into your vison?

Now you have a social media strategy it is time to take another look at your main aims for things that aren't the internet. A lovely civic social media profile probably isn't something that is going to make it into your vision. Yet many of the things in your vision will benefit from some online exposure. Over the next page or two you can review your vision.

Crack on with your vision

Your vision statement should be made up of three sections. You want to take each of these sections and think about what you could do to achieve those aims. This will probably take a fair amount of paper, so make sure you have a pad handy.

Brainstorm for each idea. There will be many things you can do to implement each one. Try not to limit yourself – no idea is a bad idea. Jot it down even if it is wildly implausible. Move on to the next section once you have exhausted your imagination. Remember no idea is a bad idea.

What do you do with all these notes?

Once you have done all three sections then you will have to narrow down your ideas. You won't be doing this just yet but it is perfectly natural for some to start to become favourites. You probably had a few ideas that you wanted to pursue before you started. That is OK but make sure you aren't rigidly sticking with them and ignoring some great alternatives.

In the end you only want to be working on about three projects for each section of your vision. So in time you will narrow it down to around five options. You don't want too many projects as you will need to run them past several people at the council. If you have loads the meetings will take all day.

For the moment it's not a bad idea to glance through these lists again when you have a second. Don't start pruning just yet but give each idea some thought. Ask yourself these questions:

- Does this idea really advance your vision?

- Can you achieve this idea?

- Do you have the time for this idea?

- Do you have the skills for this idea?

- Is this idea worth the effort?

Little steps

Being civic leader can be intimidating but it is like learning a language. You can't expect to do it in one go – that is why you have broken it down into little chunks. The same is true of starting to shine online. It is amazing what you can achieve with ten minutes a day.

What to do now

What are your online skills?

- Work out where your talents lie and where you will do your best work. Think about how you can use what you have.

What do you want to achieve?

- Make sure you are completely clear about what you are aiming for. This will stop you wasting time on social media.

What is the current incumbent doing?

- Make the most of anything you can build on but think hard if they are successful in a place you don't have the skills and interest for.

Develop a strategy

- Do the thinking and fill out the form. Then find some help to implement your strategy if you need it.

ALIGNMENT

Aligning Everyone's Expectations

You get respect when you give respect.

Michael Nutter, Mayor of Philadelphia 2008-2016

Walking the talk

Becoming a civic leader is like learning a language and you are well past the beginner classes. In fact, your vocabulary is really beginning to build. But the skill of learning a language is not just to learn the words but know how to use them. And you can get overwhelmed wondering how you are going to translate what you have learnt into the real world. This is common, but don't worry because you have been working in a systematic way. Soon it will all slot together and you will begin to feel fluent and once you can speak like a leader people will listen.

Support is great, support is what you would like. Seldom in politics do you get what you would like.

Sometimes a lack of hindrance is what you truly need. You don't mind if people aren't supporting you, so long as they aren't actively working against you. It *is* a good place to be. It can also be a hard place to get to. It requires leg work, the old-fashioned graft of meeting people and getting their opinions. And those meetings are not all easy. Ultimately it isn't pleasant when people attack the ideas you have spent time developing.

It is not pleasant but it is worthwhile because if you have an agreement over your plans you wouldn't get any nasty surprises. When you are about to launch a vital part of your programme you want to know that there won't be any objections. Support is great and many of your fellow councillors will support you, but never underestimate the value of not having people trying to derail what you are doing.

Aligning everyone's expectations

Moving from what you want to see to what you are going to do

- You are about to stop looking at the why and start grasping the how.

How to speak about what you want to do

- The focus of what you say will play a huge part in shaping people's expectations.

How to build relationships

- By now you should be getting good at relationships.

Who to talk to first?

- The order you approach the problem in will have a big impact.

Who do you need to talk to?

- You don't need to talk to all the people but you do need to talk the right people.

How to handle objections

- There will be objections, it is simply a matter of what you do with them.

Moving from what you want to see to what you are going to do

Revisit your vision statement

You may be entirely happy with your vision statement or you may want to tweak it. It is OK to keep working on it so long as it doesn't become an obsession. You have got a bit more work to do on it and, ultimately, it doesn't have to be finalised until you take office but it is best not to get fanatical about it. It is worth getting right but you do have other things to do. By this time it should be about 95% there.

From vision to mission

You have already started to brainstorm ways to implement your vision. You should have come up with a long list of ideas. Look through the list: some won't inspire, some you will fall in love with. Don't worry if you aren't 100% sure which is which. You are going to prepare a list. It won't be the final list, it will be one to guide you through the upcoming discussions. What you end up doing will be different.

Consultation list

Of course your vision isn't just about you. Ultimately it is about your community but for the moment You are going to consider it in terms of your council. You will need to discuss your ideas with senior management and councillors. That is what aligning expectations is all about.

You have three areas in your vision, and for each of them, select three to five projects. This will give you a maximum of 15 projects – and that is a lot. As you may not have enough time to explain each one to the people you will be consulting you need to be a bit ruthless. Rank your three vision sections in order. Then rank the projects in order.

It is good if you can explain all your ideas to everyone you meet but that might not be possible. If they are ranked in order you will know where to start and you will make sure you talk about the things you are keen on. It may also help you clarify in your own mind which projects are most important to you.

	VISION SECTION 1	VISION SECTION 2	VISION SECTION 3
PROJECT PRIORITIES			
Project 1			
Project 2			
Project 3			
Project 4			
Project 5			

How to speak about what you want to do

It is important to make sure that everyone knows what is going on or you might jeopardise your vision, your relationships and even your time in office.

 Night mayor

A councillor got as far as being voted mayor at the meeting before the AGM. They were all set to take office until they told some colleagues that, as an atheist, they were not going to appoint a chaplain. When the AGM arrived they found another councillor was to be elected as mayor. Don't surprise people last minute. Make sure they know.

A vision in one line

You will need to quickly tell people about your vision. You could use your prepared speeches but even a thirty-second summary is too long. You need a vision in one line. So start by looking at the different sections of your vision statement. As an example, my vision statement was as follows:

"I want to live in a town with a visible and caring local council. I want to live in a town with a vibrant community that young people want to be a part of. I want our council to be connected to its community. I want to represent a town and a council we can all be proud of."

But even that's a bit long-winded. How about:

"I want the community and council to be well-connected so that everyone feels involved and everyone feels proud of our town."

It may not cover exactly everything I want to achieve but it's punchy. And when people ask what the mayor does it's much better than saying,

"stay sober enough to open the odd fete."

Your turn

It is time for you to do the same with your mission statements. This process will take time. You will create several drafts. Don't worry about leaving it for a while and coming back to it. The advantage you have is that you have already spent time getting your vision clear. This is just the last little push. Take a moment to have a go.

....

....

....

....

....

How to speak without being dogmatic

This is possibly not something politicians are used to. They like to think that they deal in certainties – but you don't want to rush in and tell people what you want to do. Keep the idea that you are asking for help at the front of your mind at all times. It is hard to be dogmatic when you are asking for assistance: you have probably never said to someone 'I'd like some help and you must help me like this'. Go into these conversations thinking that people are going to help and you won't go far wrong.

How to build relationships

Ideally you won't be a stranger to anyone you are talking to. You may even have had a great conversation with them during your fact-finding missions.

Strengthen what you have

What is the best way to strengthen a relationship? The short answer is to become a good councillor. But that is something that you can only achieve over time. There are three things that generally matter: you must care, you must show up and you must do what you say you are going to.

Care

People respond well if you are committed to what you do. Sometimes you need to show people your passion. Remember to be passionate when you speak both formally and informally. Show them you care.

Show up

If you don't go to meetings people will think you don't care. But there is more to it than that. Being present is powerful. If you are there, people will remember you. If you are there, people will get to know you. Presence builds relationships.

Do what you say you are going to do

People want to work with people who are reliable. They don't want to work with people that aren't. It is strange but if you say you *cannot* do something people will react better than if you say you can but you only do 90% of it. Expectations are important. Make sure you don't disappoint.

It is simple. Show that it matters, show you are committed and show you are worthy of people's trust.

How can you help the council?

Another great way to strengthen your relationships is to be useful. Your vision should enhance the work of the council and therefore be useful to councillors. If you can show people how your program will benefit them it will strengthen that relationship. Look through your ideas and ask the following questions:

- How does it advance the council's aims?

- Does this make the council look good?

- Does it solve a problem the council has?

- Does it help the councillors or staff?

If what you are doing meets these criteria then people will fall over themselves to help you.

Who to talk to first?

You began to think about who to talk to earlier in the chapter about your council. You will need to think back to the work you did then. Has the strength of your relationships with key people changed at all? Have you managed to increase your standing with some people? Do you have a better connection with others than you thought?

Where to start?

There are lots of variables. You need to talk to people with influence but you also need to talk to people with whom you have a relationship. As you can't make people you already have a relationship with more influential you need to improve your relationships with the people who are already influential.

Of course this doesn't mean that now you are a civic leader you shouldn't concern yourself with the lowly people. Far from it, they will be able to help you in their own way, it is just for this exercise you need to develop your relationships with the movers and shaker. You are going to have to talk to some of, but not all, these people.

- Your political group leader

- The council leader

- The Chief Executive of the council

- A senior staff member

- The civic office manager

- Your PA

Spend a moment or two putting the people from above onto this list. Just in case you are wondering your PA has a lot of influence.

High relationship/High influence ....

....

High relationship/Mid influence ....

....

Mid relationship/High influence ....

....

Low relationship/High influence ....

....

Meeting people from the council

Previously you built relationships by using people's desire to help others. You will continue to do this. If you ask someone for advice on your strategy they are unlikely to complain about what they advised you to do. Here are how your meetings might progress:

A sample script

Obviously you are not expected to print this out and follow it word for word – this is not a call centre. But your conversations should unfold like this:

- Ask if it is a good time to talk

- Make sure they know you value their opinion

- Briefly state your vision

- Outline your most important ideas for implementation

- Make a note of their opinions

- Make a note of any project ideas they have

- If appropriate discuss the rest of your ideas

- Thank them for their time

As you are putting forward suggestions you don't have to argue the point if they don't like them. It isn't worth pushing back if they are unhappy with your ideas. The purpose is to build relationships, not to create conflict.

Make a note of what they don't like and move on. In time, you can reassess your ideas if you are getting a lot of criticism or you can work out how to counter the objections.

They will definitely offer you some ideas for implementing your vision. Some will be rubbish and some will be great. Thank them, make a note and move on. You will also meet people who are critical of what you are trying to achieve. It is tedious but if you approach them correctly they will consider themselves a valued colleague whose opinion you respect. This will do you more good than disagreeing with them.

Give it a go

Phone up a councillor who you get on with particularly well. They don't have to be influential and they don't have to be on the list of people you need to talk to. Just have a chat with them about what you want to do. Consider it a practice run.

Who do you need to talk to?

Your group leader

If your political group leader is not the leader of the council you will certainly need to talk to them. After all it is just polite.

You should take what they say with a pinch of salt. You must remember that they may well be more interested in how your program can benefit the party. This shouldn't be your motivation. Nevertheless you want to keep on good terms because their support is important.

The council leader or a cabinet member

It is sensible to give them an idea of what you are hoping to achieve. It is far better to know if they have serious objections now. That way you can do something about it. If the senior councillors are happy then in theory all the councillors should adopt your program. That said, you have probably been in politics long enough to know that the theory is rarely the practice. Getting the council leader on board is a big step but there will be other objections to handle.

Chief Executive or other senior council staff

In some ways they are better placed to advise you on what will or won't cause problems than the council leader. They may even be a great source of ideas. Just be aware that, given their position, they may be a little more guarded. They may wish to advise rather than inspire.

Always aim for the top of the tree. If you are having difficulties speak to a senior staff member; they may be able to give you a route to the Chief Exec.

The civic office manager

If you have a team manager they will be expecting to meet you to discuss your plans. That will make this easier. They may have a time of year in mind when they would like to do it. Just ask. They'll also have a process for going through everything so let them lead the meeting. Just make sure you pick up anything they have not covered.

The most important person is your secretary

It is important to be clear with your secretary. You should let them know what you are trying to do. Think about what they will be involved in. Ask them how they think that might work.

Run through the diary system again. Make sure you understand it properly. It is also worth making sure that both of you are completely clear about what you expect of each other. I cannot say this often enough. If you annoy your PA it *will* be a hard year.

That is a lot of meetings

Exactly how many meeting you need will vary. Just to make sure you are clear, make a list. You can also start to think about which order to meet them in. Start with the people you have the best relationship and then build from there.

You shouldn't need to arrange more than six meetings: two senior councillors, two senior staff and two from the civic team. But you might get it down to one senior councillor, one senior staff and one from the civic team. These meetings should give you an idea about whether there will be any objections. Better still, they will point you in the direction of any good opportunities that you might have missed.

A constantly evolving list of ideas

You will start this process with a set of ideas. It would be surprising if you finish it with the same list. When you talk to people they will have different view to yours. Sometimes they will rave about ideas that you thought where OK and these ideas may thus increase in importance. Some people will hate your plans and these ideas may drop down the list.

Best of all people will suggest new ideas. Some will be rubbish but some will be good and they will jump onto the list. Some may go straight to the top. The list will change. And this is good: It will get better, and stronger, as it changes.

How to handle objections

Sometimes objections are helpful. Sometimes they are not. Sometimes people will object to things that are important – not simply important to you but the key to achieving your main aim. Remember that not everyone understands that. Not everyone has your vision.

Sometimes you must ignore what people say. Sometimes you must do what you know to be right. True, if everyone says the idea stinks it may not be the right thing to do: if both the leader and the CEO are telling you there's no way you should even think about doing something then you should listen. But then again they might be wrong. Are you prepared to back your instincts?

	MEETING PLANNER		
	NAME	PRIORITY	DATE
Group Leader			
Council Leader			
Cabinet Member			
Chief Executive			
Other Senior Staff			
Civic Team Manager			
Secretary			

Sometimes you must push past the objections. You need to make the call. Ask yourself these questions:

- Can you get past these objections?

- Is this a fight that you can win?

- Do you need the help of the people that are objecting?

- Is there another way which may not attract complaints?

- Is this the one fight you want to take up?

- Is the outcome worth the effort?

If these questions make you nervous then maybe it is not the right project for you. If you must pursue this project then you will need to try to counter the objections. This is easier with people who you have a relationship with. You explain to them why you need to do it and why you think it will succeed. They may not end up agreeing with you but if they respect you and the general aims of your vision hopefully they will support you.

If you don't have a great relationship with someone but need their help then you will have to be more careful. Spend some time really fleshing out the idea and make sure that it is solid. You will want to discuss it thoroughly with a trusted ally. They will help work through the objections.

Once you are ready you can begin to convince people. This may require another round of meetings. Hopefully you will only need to catch up with a couple of people but if you need to see more then make the time.

Picking your fights

Sometimes in politics, as in life, you must stand up for what you want to do. The thing to remember is that you should pick your fights. You shouldn't compromise because it makes life easier but neither should you start a fight for the sake of it. There is always a tension between what you want to do and what the council want you to do. Walking that fine line is the skill of leadership.

I *cannot* overstate this because it is a lesson I learned the hard way.

Pick your fights and don't waste time and energy on things that are not important. Because time and energy are in short supply.

Reflect on what you have learned

Spend some time thinking about what people have said. Consider how you can counter their objections. Ask yourself if the idea is important enough to start a fight over. Think about how you could compromise.

Eventually your ideas will be plans and you will have to really start spreading the word. But remember that work will be a lot easier because of the groundwork you are doing now. You are concentrating on aligning everyone's expectations now because you don't want any surprises latter.

What to do now

Continue the process of going from vision into mission

- Spend some time moving from what you want to see to what you are going to do. Begin to think about how you are going to explain it to others.

Refine your vision

- Now you should be able to drop it into a conversation. Practice and refine your thirty second vision. Begin to create a vision in one line.

How can you help the council?

- Think about how you can reframe what you want to do in terms of how it can help the council.

Who do you need to talk to?

- Think about your council and who the most influential people are. Then work out what order to talk to them in.

Have some meetings

- Get them started as soon as you can.

Working with the Media

Making a connection

You have been meeting a lot of people. You have been discussing your ideas with them. You have been asking for their help and support. This is progress. It represents huge steps closer to being prepared. Doubtless there has been some conflict. Doubtless it hasn't always been pleasant. Doubtless it hasn't always felt like progress. But progress it is. It is far better to have an uncomfortable discussion now than it is while you are in office. It is better to get the disagreements straightened out now rather than let them erupt as arguments during the busiest year of your life.

Now you need to focus on the press. The media offers you much more than a chance to get your message in front of people, it lets you get yourself in front of people. You can transport yourself into people's work place, their homes and even get on their bus to work. You can say hello to thousands of people at a time. But with that comes some anxiety. There is an understandable fear of saying something wrong. After all the last thing you want to do is make yourself look silly in front of all those people. That is why most people are afraid of appearing in the media.

What you need to concentrate on is how you can prepare in a way that helps you get over the fear because the rewards of media coverage are great. If you do it right you can spread your message to thousands of people. If you craft your message properly you can communicate your vision to a much broader section of your community. The media is a great platform, jump on it.

Working with the Media

How to start a media campaign
- First things first, what do you have to do before anything else?

How to build relationships in the media
- Again you will need to focus on relationships

How to prepare for interviews
- A bit of preparation goes a long way, if you do it right.

How to look and sound good in the media
- You may not be vain but you still don't want to look and sound awful.

How to write press releases
- A press release is a magic piece of paper that transports your message far and wide.

How to manage your reputation
- It is much easier to maintain your reputation that it is to repair it.

How to start a media campaign

Before you do anything you need to find out what your council's policy is on speaking to the media. If you talk to a journalist in a personal capacity as an elected member then they can't complain. Those are your opinions and if you want to commit political suicide then that is your own business.

If, however, you are speaking as a civic leader then you are speaking on behalf of the council. In which case you will need to be more careful about what you say. Your council may wish for you to go through the press office before you start booking yourself interviews on the Graham Norton Show.

It may seem an unnecessary burden but it is better not to make enemies in the communication department. Before you do anything find out what your council expects of you. Speak to your civic office, they will know.

How to build relationships in the media

There is a lot of value in connecting with people in the media. If you build relationships with them you will be able to build a relationship with their readers, listeners or viewers. Connecting with one person allows you to connect with many. You will be using the skills you use every day to engage them.

Always give

It is difficult being a local journalist. They work hard and they are under a lot of pressure. The best way to build relationships with them is to help them achieve what they need. If you help them, they will help you. If you are easy to work with they will be easy to work with. You both win.

There are two things you can do to make life easier for them. Firstly, always make yourself available. Journalists often need quotes and information at short notice. If you are there for them they will appreciate it. Give journalists your private phone number; don't make them go through your secretary. If they leave a message call back promptly.

Secondly, try to offer them a story or extra information. If you come across something newsworthy always let your local contacts know. You could even tell them about events that you are attending. You aren't going to be able to write a press release but if you come across something interesting let your contacts know. It is best to call them but even a quick email can be helpful.

Who do you know?

The chances are you already know some people in the local media. Have you come across any journalists as a part of your council work? If you have then how can you strengthen this relationship? Could you call to tell them you are going to take office? If you feel comfortable doing this, pick up the phone. They will be covering a lot of things you will be doing. If you ask them how you can best help then they will realise you will be easy to work with.

Even if you don't know any local journalists you do know someone that does. Several of your fellow councillors will have good contacts and information. Which councillors could you call who could tell you about your local journalists? What can they tell you about those journalists' interests? Could they even make some introductions for you?

How to prepare for interviews

> **Quick Win**
>
> Get in touch. You could start a relationship or get a valuable introduction.

The success of your interview will depend on how much preparation you put in. The more effort you make the better you will come across. The more time you spend crafting your message the easier it will be for you to get it across.

When you agree to an interview make sure you know what it will be about. Get as much information as you can, then spend some time thinking about the subject and what your message will be. If you have the time it is a good idea to look at some past publications, episodes or their website. This will give you an idea of the style of the interview and what kind of questions they ask.

In an ideal world all interviews would be an opportunity for you to promote your vision. Sadly, the media is not simply a vehicle for your message. Sometimes you will have to talk about stories or subjects and you won't be able to think of a way to easily discuss your vision. When that happens you need to work out a different way to benefit your council or your community.

In situations like this there is no substitute for mental heavy lifting. You are going to have to do some thinking about what you are going to say. If you are totally stuck then do some reading around the subject. Pull up a few websites and see what comes to mind. This will obviously help you answer the questions but it will also get you thinking and you may well be able to come up with an approach to the subject.

To begin with you should list out the key point of your message. Once you have a few ideas you may need to do some research to expand them. Or you may want to come back to them later. You often do your best thinking when you aren't thinking about it at all. After a bit of musing some ideas will come to the fore and others will fade.

Once you are happy with your key points you will have to get to know them. Practice saying them out loud. Try to use them to answer different questions so you are comfortable with talking about them in different ways. These ideas will need to roll off your tongue, and if you keep practicing you will find that this happens quickly enough.

The inauguration interview

You can't always tell what the media will ask you about. That is because you can't be sure what will happen during your year. One thing that you know will happen is that you will take office, so it makes sense to prepare for interviews about taking office.

In an ideal world you would have a good friend who has lots of PR and media experience that can help you prepare for interviews. If you haven't then you will need to find someone who likes you enough to be truthful and critical when needed. Ask them nicely to interview you using the questions at the bottom of this section.

How to run a good practice interview

Try to imagine that it is a real interview. Take it seriously and try to give full answers. You could get them to phone you when you aren't expecting it and do the interview on the hoof. This is more realistic as it is what happens in the real world. You could also record the interview so you can go over it in a debrief session.

Try not to look at the questions in the next section. Admittedly, this makes showing them to the person who will interview you a bit tricky. Even if you do sneak a peek they will probably change them and they will certainly adapt them to their own style.

Just like in a real interview try to anticipate the questions that you will be asked. Try to work out what you want to say, you will want to mention your vision and it will be great if you have the odd killer line like, 'we can't change the world but we can bring our community together'. Make sure you can get this into the interview. You won't be able to anticipate everything but if you have done your preparation you will breeze through.

Practice interview questions

Here are some suggested practice questions. They are by no means exhaustive so please add new ones. They are also quite generic so you are encouraged to put them into your own words.

- What are you looking forward too?

- What are you hoping to achieve?

- Can you tell me a little bit more about yourself?

- How have you prepared for the office?

- What skills will you bring from other areas of your life?

- Do you have a theme for your year?

- What do you think will be the biggest challenge?

When you ask these questions make some notes so you can give good feedback. Cover what went well but also try to make suggestions for improvement.

How to look and sound good in the media

Tips for TV

It used to be only the lucky few civic leaders that made it on to television but with more channels and particularly more local television the opportunity for screen time is increasing.

Talking to the camera is hard. It tends to suck the life out of any performance. Generally, this is because when you talk to a camera it gives you nothing in return. Even a low-key audience will give you a reaction. To counter this, you will need to raise the enthusiasm levels. It is easier talking to a host because they will smile and nod. It also helps if you can build a rapport with them.

You need to be a careful about what you wear. Televisions have improved so you won't need to avoid stripes but you must still ensure that what you wear looks good and make you feel confident. Pick your outfit the night before. If you aren't certain check it with someone you trust. Just make sure it is ready in plenty of time. The morning of your big interview is no time to find out that your favourite dress needs washing.

Tips for Radio

Always go to the studio if you can. You won't always be invited; sometimes radio stations will send someone to your house and sometimes they will record you over the phone. Ask if you can come to the studio. Being interviewed face-to-face helps to create a bond, making it sound more like a natural conversation.

If you are going to the radio station get there in plenty of time. This not only relaxes you but it makes a big difference to the show's producer. They don't want to be biting their fingernails about whether you are going to show up or not. Remember you are trying to make their lives easier and to come across as a good guest. If you do they will ask you back.

You should always dress smartly for the radio. Sure, none of the listeners will see – but the staff will. More importantly it creates the right feeling in you. Professional dress, professional attitude.

Try to create an affinity with the host – this is, after all, the purpose of doing it live. If you engage them it will sound like two old friends chatting. Smile throughout the interview: it will come across in your voice. Finally, when you have finished make sure you thank everyone. It is likely there will be a break after your interview for a trailer or advert so take the opportunity to thank the host. Then thank the producer and offer your services should they need anything in the future.

In the comfort of your own home

If you are being interviewed at home you need to take it as seriously as if you are going in to the studio. Make sure you are by the phone in plenty of time before the call. If you have a home office this is the place to be. Otherwise somewhere that is quiet and free from distractions will do; just make sure you are comfortable.

If you are a bit unsure of your message it is OK to use notes. Have them as bullet points on cards. Resist the temptation to write things out long form. Nothing sucks the life out of your performance like reading from a script.

If you are at home and have some time alone before the interview the chances are that you won't be speaking much. It isn't a bad idea to do some vocal warm-ups before taking the call. You don't have to do anything too complex – just make sure that you have done some talking before you are heard by thousands of people.

You don't like your voice

Yes, you hate your voice. Everyone does. It is because hearing it recorded is different to hearing it when you are speaking. It is all to do with the way sound travels. This is very interesting but the important thing is to not get hung up on it. You are not the only one.

You can spend a lot of time and money trying to make your voice sound brilliant but you don't need to employ a vocal coach. All you really need is a bit of enthusiasm.

Trust the photographer

Photos are a big part of local journalism. Lots of bright colour photos communicate the feeling of an event brilliantly. And it is cheaper to pay someone to take a photo than it is to pay someone to write a thousand words.

Either way you are going to get photographed a lot. This is great because it helps to promote you and what you are doing. You should remember that taking exciting and visually arresting photos is a skill. It is a skill that takes years to learn and it is a skill you don't have. So when photographers ask you to do things that seem stupid go with them. You aren't well placed to know whether it will produce a good photo or not. Trust them and smile. They will produce some excellent photos.

A world of subjects

Sometimes you get interviewed about an issue that is in the news but not necessarily that relevant to you. This is a good sign: they have asked you to talk about it because you are a reliable guest.

 **Night mayor**

A civic leader was asked to give an interview on the strategic defence review. This was a subject they knew nothing about. With some hard work they managed to sound knowledgeable and relate it back to their community.

Hot topic interview

The idea is simple: get a friend to pick an issue that is in the news, and then to interview you. They should tell you the subject but keep the questions to themselves.

It is worth practicing being interviewed on radio or TV so record the interview – preferably on video but audio is also fine. As it is recorded you can play it back and see what you did well – and what you can improve.

What sort of questions?

You need to think about the questions that they might ask. These are the kind of questions you should be considering:

- How will this issue affect your community?

- What is your opinion of the issue?

- What is the council going to be doing about this issue?

- How can people in the community respond to this issue?

- Will you be making this issue a priority while you are in office?

Obviously, some questions will be specific to the subject and you can only work those out by thinking about the subject and doing some research.

Record for radio or TV

Ideally you will video the practice interview. You might think that this is difficult, but the quality isn't important. If you can see and hear yourself it is OK. The simplest way to record it is on a digital camera or smartphone. You could also use the camera that is built into your laptop. Recording sound is even easier. You could use a laptop or just the voice recorder on your phone.

Once you have recorded the mock interview look back through it a few times and ask yourself how you could improve. You could make some notes of your areas for improvement to guide you through the real thing.

How to write Press Releases

A press release is short statement sent to journalists to tell them about your event, celebration or announcement. Writing a them is both easy and difficult. There is not much to them but getting it all right is a real skill.

For the best results you shouldn't just fire off press releases: you should think about what you are trying to achieve. Before writing anything ask yourself these questions.

- What do you hope the coverage will achieve?

- Do you want to raise awareness, get help or sell tickets?

- Is there anything about it that is of more than local interest?

- What is the time frame for what you hope to accomplish?

Once you've worked out what you want to achieve then you need to find the right media outlets to send your release to. When looking at possible options ask yourself these questions:

- What kind of articles or features do they have regularly?

- What is their style - formal or informal, jovial or serious?

- Which audience are they aiming at?

- Does it fit your image or focus?

- Will they be interested in your story?

Your press release should be framed in a way that interests their audience. This will increase your chances of getting an article published. Once you have worked out what you are aiming at you can start on the release.

The press release

Try to keep it to a minimum: one page is enough. Don't add loads and loads of information. If the journalist needs more, they will call.

Catchy headline

It must be seriously catchy. If it is dull they stop reading. Add a subheading if you need to but keep it less than 18 words.

Attention-grabbing paragraph

Start with the name of your city or town and the date of the event. Then get straight to the point. It only needs a few sentences so make them the best you have.

Body paragraph

This paragraph should include all the essential information. You want to answer the who, what, why, where and when questions. Put the most important stuff first. This may be all that they read. Expand on the first section with a little bit more information. Write in short punchy sentences. Make it clear. Keep it exciting.

Quote paragraph

Include some quotes that provide insight into what you are doing. They will probably be from you but you can add other relevant people. They shouldn't include facts and figures; those belong in the body paragraph.

For Immediate Release

Write this below the last paragraph. Unless it isn't. Then write when it's embargoed until.

Contact details

You need to add phone and email details for your main contact. It must be someone who is available and can answer questions. The only thing worse than no-one answering is someone answering who has no clue.

Boilerplate

Finally, add a short biography of you and your vision. This allows people to understand how the event sits within your whole year. For example my boiler plate would read like this:

"Duncan Bhaskaran Brown was born and raised in Abingdon. He's proud to be its youngest mayor. During his time in office he hopes to meet as many people from the town as possible and maybe even inspire a few young people to become more involved in their community."

 Twenty-first century mayor

"Lord Mayor in bed with beauty queen". That got your attention. Rae Humberstone, Lord Mayor of Oxford opened a hotel with Miss Oxford, Shirin O'Neil. This eye-catching headline generated plenty of interest.

Sending it

Use your punchy title as the subject line. If it is dull they won't even open the email. Don't send it as an attachment; paste the release into the email making it easy to read. You will need to send it when it is news worthy. If you are reacting to something that has happened send it as soon as you can but if it is about an event in the future send it around five days ahead.

Practice a press release

Pick an event that you are going to organise. Use the templates below to create a press release. You won't have all the information you need so write it as you would like the event to happen.

Once it is done leave it for a week before reviewing it. After tweaking it show it to the person who helped with the practice interviews. When the event comes around don't forget about it. If you dig it out you will have a head start on the promotion.

PRESS RELEASE TEMPLATE		
Catchy headline:		
Event name:	**Town or city:**	**Date:**
Attention grabbing paragraph:		
Body paragraph:		
Quote paragraph:		
For immediate release or embargoed until:		
Contact details:		
About you:		

How to manage your reputation

It is easier to maintain a good reputation than it is to try and rebuild one. Don't get caught doing something that you will regret seeing in the paper.

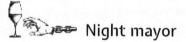 ## Night mayor

The following things have appeared in the media recently.

- A mayor saying the public will foot the bill for their parking ticket

- A mayor swearing at people on Facebook

- A mayor causing a traffic jam by parking illegally while going to a shop

- A deputy mayor saying that prayer was a 'gay cure'

I could go on.

The press loves stupid civic leaders; they will go to town on them. So be careful whilst you are in office. Here are some hints:

- Don't say anything stupid on social media

- Emails are not private

- Stay sober

- Never say "don't you know who I am?"

- Don't do anything you don't want to see on the front page of the local paper

- If you get caught, resign

The bottom line is that if you always act with integrity you will be OK. That is the best advice there is.

What is in your closet?

Before you take office it is a good idea to take a moment to think if there is anything that might come back to haunt you.

- Do you have any unresolved financial issues?

- Is there anything on your social media sites that is inappropriate or would make you uncomfortable if it came to light?

- Do you have any pending legal or tax issues?

- Is there anything in your life that you won't want all your friends to find out about?

If any of these questions make you squirm then it is time to take some action. It is better to deal with it now than when it is in the papers.

You will get that call

The media needs something to talk about and it may as well be you. To do that you will need to do what you do all the time: build relationships and be clear about your message. That is why twenty-first century mayors are so media-friendly.

What to do now

Who do you know in the local media?

- Make some calls and start to build those relationships.

The inauguration interview

- Get a good friend to help you with the practice interview. You could get them to call you out of the blue to give it a proper press interview feel.

Hot topic interview

- Get your interview friend to help you with this. Record it and watch it back to review your performance.

Practice a press campaign

- Use the template to develop a release. Review it then show it to your trusted friend.

Protect your reputation

- Commit to not doing anything stupid during your time in office. Make sure there is nothing outstanding that could come back to haunt you.

PLANNING

From Vision to Mission

"Mayors are judged by results".

Willie Brown, Mayor of San Francisco 1996-2004

Seeing is important

You are nearly there, you can see the finish line. You are in this position because you have done so much. You have put in a huge amount of effort and that is why the finishing line is so close. But even having only a short distance to go can be stressful. Those last few steps are often the hardest. Even if you don't have much to do, you may still be wondering where you will find the time to finish. That is quite normal. Just concentrate on the destination. Think about all the benefits of being prepared: the confidence, the clarity, the skills and the support.

Those last few steps of the journey are some of the most important of all. You are going to turn your vision into plans. This process will give you a clear idea of what you are going to do. This clarity will help you throughout your time in office by giving you the ability to see whether something will help you or it won't. Of course it isn't going to come without some effort on your part. It will take work to transform your strategy into tactics. Even talking through your plans with your team will take effort. Planning doesn't just happen.

But clear plans are invaluable because they give confidence. If you know that what you want to do is not just a vague aspiration, but a detailed plan you will be self-assured. It will give you confidence in your ideas, confidence in your actions, even confidence in your team. And confidence helps but it is planning that makes your dreams possible.

From Vision to Mission

Finish the talking before you do the planning

- Get everything straight before you plan too much.

Which ideas do you want to concentrate on?

- You may want to do it all but please remember it is only a year.

Beginning the long plan

- You are going to get more detailed, you are going to get nitty gritty.

Planning the year

- It is a good idea to figure out how these plans fit into the time available.

Developing the one-page civic plan

- Detail has a place but it is time for one final overview.

Finish the talking before you do the planning

Have you spoken to everyone at your council? You may not have had the chance yet. That is OK. There is a lot to do. But you should make sure you have scheduled meetings to catch up with the last few. You can't really move from your initial ideas to concrete plans until you have.

If you have spoken to everyone, great. What was the result? Are they full of support or will there be significant flack? Sometimes you must fight for what you believe in. Sometimes you must stand against the objections. It is OK to do that for something important or something that your whole program depends on.

If it is not vital then it is not worth fighting for. Think carefully before you start taking on the whole council. Take another look at this list of questions about aligning everyone's expectations.

- Can you get past these objections?

- Is this a fight that you can win?

- Do you need the help of the people that are objecting?

- Is there another way which may not attract complaints?

- Is this the one fight you want to take up?

- Is the outcome worth the effort?

If you can honestly go through that list without wanting to give up on the idea then it is the right thing for you to do. You should work out how to counter the objections and win the arguments. Make sure that these discussions happen behind closed doors. You don't want to turn your role into a platform for slinging mud.

 Night mayor

A civic leader managed to pick a fight with other councillors about once a fortnight. Needless to say she was unpopular - even within her own party. She lost the support of many people just because she didn't know how to pick her fights.

Have you recruited all the team?

It is a good idea to have your team in place before you get too far into the planning phase. Mostly this is because you shouldn't plan until you know what you have got to work with. Maybe you are expecting to have help that will free up a lot of your time. If that help never materialises then you will need to change your plans to fit the time you have.

There is more. If you recruit someone who is enthusiastic they will suggest ways of doing things that you had not thought of. This may well save you time and effort. So it is better not to finalise your plans until you've discussed them with your team. You must be careful, though. If they suggest a lot of new projects then you will need to go back and talk to a lot of councillors and staff. You probably don't have the time to do that. Let them contribute but make sure you keep a clear direction.

What do you do if you haven't recruited everyone?

If you are finalising your team then it is straightforward. You should go off and put the last pieces in place. If, however, you are struggling to fill a role you need then you have an issue. If you think through all of the groups of people you know then a candidate may come to mind. It may be useful to ask around. Who do you know that might know someone who could help?

Ultimately, if you can't find an essential recruit you may need to rethink your vision. It is a fine balance. You don't want to drop things you are passionate about but then you don't want to give yourself too much to do. Think about these questions:

- Can you adapt the project?

- Is there another way of implementing what you want to?

- Can you split up the strategy and the implementation?

- Could someone in your team take on an additional responsibility?

- If you took something else off your plate could you do it?

Hard questions, but it is better to think about them now than when you are in the middle of the melee.

Which ideas do you want to concentrate on?

More ideas than you need?

You should have more ideas than you need. You started off with five for each of your vision sections. You should have picked up a few more during your conversations at the council. They should all be tolerable to the people you have to work with. You might have one that you are prepared to fight for but they should all be broadly acceptable.

That doesn't mean that they are all possible. That doesn't mean you have the time to do them all. You now need to really home in on which ones are right: which ones best serve your purpose?

The ideas barometer

You are going to assess your ideas to see which ones you should concentrate on and which you should discard or rethink.

Look through your three vision sections with their five projects. Start by asking this simple question: can you make this project happen? If you can't then the idea needs a rethink or it goes in the bin. If there is a way you can make it happen put it onto the table below.

Address each question for each project. If you can answer yes then put a tick in the box. Finally add all the ticks up to give each project a score out of six.

PROJECT	Do you have the time to complete this idea?	Will this idea benefit the council or community?	Can you make this idea a success?	Will this idea get you closer to your goal?	Is the benefit worth the energy expended?	Does this idea fit into your overall vision?	Total score out of six

THE IDEAS BAROMETER

Ideally all the projects that you take forward would score six out of six. If none do then you may want to do some thinking about whether these are the right projects. If some score strongly and others don't then your choice is clear. If they all score highly try doing the exercise again, only be a bit more ruthless.

If something that you have your heart set on doesn't sit well on the barometer then you may want to rethink it. Ask yourself how you can adapt it to get around the problems that you have just uncovered.

Beginning the long plan

Once you have decided on your main projects it is time to develop more detailed plan. To do this You are going to keep breaking things down in to smaller sections. You started by coming up with loads of ideas for your vision and then narrowing it down to three sections. Then you broke down each vision section into five or so projects.

Now you need to break these projects down further. You are aiming to make them into smaller and smaller chunks. Soon enough you have turned a complex and difficult project into a series of achievable steps. But these steps on their own are not enough. You need some more details.

For this you are going to use a form which I like to call the 'action one-sheet'. This is primarily because it gets all the actions onto one sheet. There is one in the workbook which you can find here: www.theciviccoach.com/mtc-workbook/. This might be a good time to print off a few. Before you look at an example here are the sections that it contains.

Vision section

What you are setting out to achieve. Make sure it is short and clear.

Project

Each project should be clear and singular. While it will be part of your overall vision it should stand alone. If it relies too much on other things then maybe it should be a part of a bigger project rather than one in its own right.

Area

The areas are what you need to do to make the project happen. Again they should be clear and singular. If they seem too big or ill-defined break them down into several areas.

Task

The tasks are the lowest level on the action one-sheet. They should be the nitty-gritty of what you are going to do. This should be the kind of things that you can arrange in a day or two. If these tasks are too big then they need to be further broken down – but don't break them down so much that you could achieve them in a few minutes.

Who will help?

You are not going to make this happen on your own so you will need to make a note of who will be helping you and what areas they will be looking after. There will be overlap between people but try to keep it as clear as possible.

When will it happen?

This is where you put the key dates that things need to be done by. This is perhaps the most important section. Make sure you allow a bit of time for slippage and problems. You do not want to be doing it all last minute.

What will you need?

Here you will document the major resources you will need to make things happen. You don't need to get so detailed that you know exactly how many paperclips you require. Just make sure you have got down anything that is important, expensive or difficult to get hold of.

ACTION ONE-SHEET

Project:		Date:	

Vision Line:

AREA 1		AREA 2	
Task 1		Task 1	
Task 2		Task 2	
Task 3		Task 3	
AREA 3		AREA 4	
Task 1		Task 1	
Task 2		Task 2	
Task 3		Task 3	
AREA 5		AREA 6	
Task 1		Task 1	
Task 2		Task 2	
Task 3		Task 3	
Who will help?		**Tasks**	

Immediate:
Short term:
Medium term:
Long term:
What will you need?

Now it is your turn

It is time to start filling out action one-sheets for all the projects you have developed. This will end up being around ten to fifteen action one–sheets – a considerable job of work. Try to get them filled out over the next couple of weeks. Don't be tempted to miss a few out. The ones that you don't want to do are almost certainly the ones that you need to do some work on. Get printing, start filling them out, they will help.

What else do you have to do?

During your initial conversations with council-members you should have got a good idea of what is expected of you during your time in office. Some of these things will have become a part of your vision. Some of them may seem to be a distraction from it. Either way you will have to take them into consideration during your planning.

You are looking for the big things that involve you taking a lead in the organisation. If you aren't interested in these, maybe you can delegate them. It is important to note that although you may be able to delegate the work you will still have to live with the result. This means that you should plan to the work just as much as you would with your other big events. You will need to make sure that these tasks are performed in a manner that you are happy with. So plan them, delegate them and keep an eye on them.

It is also worth having a quick look back over the diary exercise. Check to make sure that you have not missed anything big. Events that are simply going to be busy days can be left on the diary: it is events that will require some hard work that you are interested in.

Once you are sure that you have made a note of all of them, fill out an action one-sheet for each. Add these to your other action one-sheets. Even if these are things that you aren't particularly keen on doing it is important to make sure they are done well. After all they are a part of what you have to do and therefore a part of how you perform your role.

Reconsidering your goals

Once you have spent some time developing your plans you may start to have some doubts about what you have taken on. This is OK. Sometimes it is only when you really get into planning something that you realise it is not the right thing for you.

If you are in any doubt, then look at the ideas barometer. Think hard about it and discuss it with your partner or someone you trust. Just remember that if you change one of your aims then you may need to change your vision accordingly.

What to do with your action one-sheets

Should you check through them constantly during your time in office? Maybe. Maybe not. People work in different ways. Maybe they are the kind of thing that will help you; maybe you will refer to them frequently, ticking off the tasks and the areas as you achieve them. Maybe you won't. You won't lose anything by trying it.

Even if don't refer to them regularly they will still help. They will force you to think about the following: what you want to achieve, how you could go about achieving it, when you might do it, who might help and what you might need. That sort of mental heavy lifting is never a waste of time.

Planning the year

Another look at your diary

You have already spent a bit of time looking at how your year will pan out. Look back to the first diary you did when you were finding out about your council and the one you looked at whilst you were planning your community strategy. You are going to add your plans to it to make sure there are no clashes.

Firstly, copy the events over to this new one. Now go through your action one-sheets and add any significant dates from those. If you need a bigger calendar it might not be a bad idea to get one of those wall planners or a sheet of A3. You could even get a bit carried away and use a whiteboard – just don't ever call your office the War Room.

This diary starts in March to give you plenty of time to prepare before you take office. Put anything you still need to do before you take office into

March or April. That way you will be as ready as you can be when the big day arrives.

	YEAR PLANNER	
MARCH	**APRIL**	**MAY**
JUNE	**JULY**	**AUGUST**
SEPTEMBER	**OCTOBER**	**NOVEMBER**
DECEMBER	**JANUARY**	**FEBRUARY**
MARCH	**APRIL**	**MAY**

If you are looking at some of the months and thinking that this amount of work isn't possible then you are probably right. You may be trying to do too much. Have a look and see what you can change. If you can, move things to a quieter time of the year. If you really can't then make sure you are delegating as much as possible. If you can't move it or delegate it then the only solution is hard work.

Just like the action one-sheets you might wonder what to do with this information. If you are the kind of person who benefits from big wall calendars then put it on the wall. You may want to put it into your diary. You could also share it with your PA. Then they can remind you not to book too many events at busy times. You could also use a website or app to organise the information.

Even if you do nothing with it at least you have thought about how the year will look. If you have merely eased congestion in one area of the year then you have done well. It comes down to the same point: this kind of thinking is never a waste of time.

Developing the one-page civic plan

The last form that you will need to fill out is a 'vision one-sheet'. This is because – you guessed it – it puts your vision onto one sheet. Some councils – those enlightened enough to have one – would call it a civic business plan. This is probably the most important exercise you will do. It is important because if you can fill it out then you are where you need to be.

CIVIC ONE-SHEET

Your vision in one line:	
Vision Section	
PROJECT 1	
Aim of project	
PROJECT 2	
Aim of project	
PROJECT 3	
Aim of project	
Vision Section	
PROJECT 1	
Aim of project	
PROJECT 2	
Aim of project	
PROJECT 3	
Aim of project	
Vision Section	
PROJECT 1	
Aim of project	
PROJECT 2	
Aim of project	
PROJECT 3	
Aim of project	

That is it in a nutshell

This form is also important because it sums up everything you have done in an easy-to-digest form. It means you can communicate the broad scope of your plan without even saying a word. While you may not want to send this actual form to people you will need to share in information on it. Copy your words from it to your word processor. Play with the formatting so that it looks good, add a bit more information if you need to but keep it to one page: it is supposed to be on one sheet. Keep it to a summary, if it isn't vital it should not be on there.

Who wants to see this?

> ### Quick Win
>
> Take a moment to reflect on everything you've done. Are you smiling? Because you should be.

You want to send this document far and wide. You should give it to the people you have been building relationships with. You shouldn't just send it to them in an impersonal fashion. Ideally you want to hand it to them so you can see their expression. The chances are they have never had a civic leader that has done anything like this before. Then again, they have probably never had a twenty-first century mayor before.

Once you have given it to the important people you should email around too. Your fellow councillors would definitely be interested in it. You should also send it to the members of your team. It is also helpful to send it to someone who can hold you accountable. Ask them to check in with you over the year to see how you are progressing.

Finally, please, please, please email it to me. I'm on info@theciviccoach. com and I would get a massive kick out of seeing it. Thank you in advance.

It is also for you

Don't forget that this document really is your plan. You should keep it at the forefront of your mind throughout the year.

Visions inspire, plans achieve

Just because planning isn't sexy doesn't mean that it isn't exciting. It will take a long time to complete all these plans for the year: it will probably take about twelve months. But things are really starting to come together, which is thrilling.

What to do now

Finish recruiting your team

- It is time to put the last few people into place. You should have in-principle agreements from people or at the very least you should have a clear idea of who you are going to ask.

Finish discussing your ideas at the council

- Once you know that your ideas won't cause any problems then you can begin to plan in more detail.

Fill out action one-sheets

- It is time to move from ideas to action. The action one-sheet will help you turn your aims into areas and tasks. It will also help you set time-scales and allocate roles.

Keep filling out action one-sheets

- This process can take a lot of work so keep at it.

Update your diary and make sure everything fits in

- Make sure that you have the time to achieve all you want. Put all the key dates and busy periods onto your dairy and rearrange things if needed.

Fill out the 'civic one-sheet'

- Collate all the information. Polish it up so it sounds beautiful. Then send it out to everyone, including me.

Life After Office

"By the time you've had a year of this you're in line for a pretty substantial holiday".

Jeffrey Mountevans, Lord Mayor of the City of London 2015-2016

More than a grin

Smile. What you have done is amazing. What you have done goes far beyond what most mayors and council chairs ever do. You are a part of a small group of people that are genuinely prepared for the role they undertake. You *are* a leader.

Now you need to take a look at what will happen when you step down. The fact that there is a clear end to your time in office is a big advantage. It gives you something to aim for and it focuses your mind. Because now you know what you have to do you and you also know when it has to be done by. That will help. But standing down is also something that can be difficult. It can be hard to adjust to life after your office. You will find that when you stand down there is a big hole in your life. It can even be depressing. Finishing is tough.

That is why it is important to spend some time thinking about what you will do when you have finished. You can't plan everything that will happen during your time in office but if you consider certain things it will put you in a better position when you stand down. Having an idea about what you will do makes the transition much more comfortable. It is time to plan the final piece of the jigsaw, and then you will be completely ready. Now that really is something to smile about.

Life after office

What to do immediately after you finish

- You need to have a smooth transition.

How to record your experience

- A lot is going to happen, you need a plan to help you remember it all.

How do you tell people about it?

- You are going to do some important work, people will want to hear about it.

How can you help your successor?

- The office continues, you want to leave it on a sound footing.

Where do you want to go now?

- It can be a great launch pad, but where to?

What to do immediately after you finish

Don't relax. It sounds strange but you can't take your foot of the gas the day you step down. There will inevitably be loose ends that need tying up. If you relax you will not get around to doing them. This means it will drag on and it will make it difficult to take the next step.

....And then relax

Leave it a few weeks, tie up any loose ends, and then take a holiday. You have earned it. You know what helps you relax, do that.

Is it like retiring?

It is tempting to use the analogy of retirement. It makes sense. You get a whole load of spare time. People will ask you if you want to use some of it to help them. The best advice is not to say yes to anything until you have had some time to get used to your new-found freedom. In that sense it is like retiring.

> **Quick Win**
>
> Put two weeks' holiday in your diary. Make sure you tell employers, family and anyone else that needs to know. Book it. Now.

Yet there is something else at play. Before you took on the role you were probably busy. With your council, sure, but also with being an active part of your community. When you took office, you put most of that on hold. When you stand down you have got a blank canvas. Aside from your responsibilities as a councillor, you could do whatever you want with your free time. In short, you will have an opportunity to reinvent your life.

How to record your experience

A record for you

You will put a lot of time and effort into being a civic leader, so it is only sensible to make some sort of record of it. There are many ways of doing this, but before you think about how that record will take shape how will you keeping track as you go along?

Keeping a diary

You may find the time to keep a detailed diary. Or you might think you can but in the end find life gets away from you. It is better to start with realistic, rather than optimistic, aims. Think about these points:

- Are you going to have time to keep a diary?

- Should it be on paper or electronic?

- Will you be able to fill it out daily?

- Would it be better to do a weekly update?

The box method

Get a box. Use it to save things like programs, leaflets and memorabilia. If nothing else, they will act as good reminders of your time in office. It is better to save these things; you can always throw them away later.

Photos

It is also important to make sure you get photos of yourself. You will want photos of all the exciting things you have done. You should try to take a camera with you – it might be time to buy a phone with a good one. If you can't get your own photos taken, try to get hold of copies of other people's pictures. In these days of digital photography this is so much easier. Just be careful about copyright. Never publish or display photos you don't have the right to.

A blog

One of the advantages of writing a blog is it can act as a perfect diary. If you write a weekly review of 500 words with two or three photos: something perfectly achievable. At the end of the year you will have a 25,000-word biographical account of your time in office, with over 100 photos to boot. Of course this will form part of your online strategy but it will also double as an amazing record.

 **Twenty-first century mayor**

The Lord Mayor of Oxford, John Goddard, managed to have his own artist accompany him to many events. She drew quick sketch impressions of what was going on and then filled in the detail later. Not every civic leader can count on such a great record but then the artist in question was his wife.

How do you tell people about it?

Have you thought about writing a book?

Before you make any inroads into writing a book you should be sure who you are writing for. There are three groups of people you might choose to produce a book for.

- Your family

- Local people

- The whole world

Your family

Today it is easier than ever to produce a book. You could get some photos and jot down impressions from your time in office, then you have several options of how to turn it into a book. You could use a company like

Photobox.com to make something more like a photo album or a website like Lulu.com that would produce more of a book.

Either option is a great way of creating something to remind you of your time in office. It will also provide a valuable addition to your family history: maybe in a 100 years' time your great-grandchildren will read your words and look at the pictures of you enjoying events.

Local people

Could you write something that would interest the local history group? Meet them and ask. Could you appeal to other local people? Visit your bookshop and pick their brains. It won't make you rich but if you are interested in putting in the time you could produce something that you are proud of.

The whole world

There are two things that can make your story a bit more bankable. One is if you happened to have a particularly interesting life before you became a civic leader. Think rags to riches: are you Dick Whittington? This may appeal to a certain section of the book-reading public. Sadly, the other way is if you were involved in some tragedy or event that made big news.

 Twenty-first century mayor

Rudy Giuliani's book is about leadership yet it is overshadowed by his experiences of 9/11. It is not that his book wouldn't have sold but the 9/11 connection massively boasted sales. 9/11 is what people are interested in.

You think you can make it work

If you think your story has broad enough appeal to sell many copies you will need to interest a publisher. To do that you shouldn't write the whole book.

Start by doing some research into publishers, your local library will have the Writers' & Artists' Yearbook and that is where you should begin. Try to find a few that have published similar book to what you are hoping to write. Check their submission guidelines and send them what they ask for. But be warned the chances are all you will get back are polite rejection letters and you might not even get those.

Trust me it is hard writing a book

Producing a quality book requires a lot of time and effort as well as the professional skills of editors, designers and artists. If you think writing a book is a get-rich-quick strategy then you are sorely mistaken. In fact, many people lose money trying to put out a book.

There are many websites and books written about writing and publishing, that is because it is complex. Before you consider self-publishing a book - in fact before you even consider writing one - you should do plenty of research to work out if it is the right thing for you.

Why not say a few words?

You will probably be asked to talk about your experiences in office. You already know several people who belong to groups that are looking for speakers. I have spoken about my experiences to countless Women's Institutes, U3As and other clubs such as Probus. I must confess I really enjoy it. Don't be put off by being asked to talk for 45 minutes. It sounds daunting but all you are doing is telling some stories. Make it conversational and the time will fly past. Just remember everything you have learned about speech making from the earlier chapter.

How can you help your successor?

You are going to be replaced

There comes a time in every civic leader's life when they have to hand over the chains of office to someone else. This is disappointing but strangely comforting: however busy it gets you know there will be an end.

All good leaders make sure someone is ready when they stand down. The first thing you need to do is find out who will take over from you. Every council is different – how will your successor be appointed? Will your deputy take over? Wonderful. Is there a candidate in line already? This is great. Will you be involved in selecting your replacement? This is also good.

Is there a mad scramble to find someone as no-one wants to do it? That is a problem. If no one is found to replace you then you might have to do another year. Is that what you want? If not then you need to start thinking about a successor.

The best laid plans

Sadly, life has a habit of getting in the way of your plans. If your council's elections are at the end of your time in office then all your strategies can quickly go awry. It is all too easy for the person that was supposed to fill your role to not hold on to their seat. Even if they do sometimes they still lose out as the ruling party changes. It happens and it is heart-breaking.

Training your successor

One way or another someone will be taking over from you. This means you have a responsibility to help ensure that they have the information, if not the skills, they need to do the job. As a civic leaders you have a responsibility to share your knowledge and offer your support to the next wave.

You are the person with the most up-to-date information about the role. All too often you will be the only person who is offering them anything. True, you can't be expected to run an in-depth training program but make sure that you try to help them any way you can.

Share with your deputy

There is a form of mayoral masochism, it is the mistaken belief that the best mayor is the one who attends the most events. This is silly as the best civic leaders are the ones that have the most impact on their community and deliver the most value for their councils.

This means you don't have to go to everything. Let your deputy do some events. This will help them get the hang of what they are supposed to do. More than that, it will give you some time to concentrate on having an impact and delivering value.

If you can make some time, discuss these events with them. Ask them what is going well and what worries them. You can be a fantastic mentor for them. And if you really like them you could buy them a copy of this book.

Your legacy

There is a selfish reason for helping your successor. You want your vision to continue. The things you do well are the things that they should be trying to emulate. The more you help them the more likely they are to continue your good work after you have stood down. Now that is an impact.

This is particularly important when it comes to social media or blogs. You don't want them to stop when you do. At the very least make sure your successor has access to any accounts or pages you have set up. You can't force them to continue what you have done but you can encourage and support them.

 **Night mayor**

There are many social media accounts that a civic leader spent a year building an audience on only for them to abruptly stop in May.

Where do you want to go now?

One of the best things about being a civic leader is that it is a great platform. It can take you to some interesting places.

Do a good job

The best thing to aim for is good memories. But if you want more then it is worth spending a minute or two thinking about the avenues that may open for you. Of course the best way to ensure that you end up where you want to be is to do a great job. Wherever you want to be, you are more likely to get there if you are good at what you do.

The next step

One of the most common career paths is to become a different type of civic leaders. There are plenty of people who have been both mayors and council chairs. This is OK – you will, after all, have the skills to fulfil the role. This might mean you need to get elected to another council but the exposure you get whilst in office should help with this.

Maybe you have eyes on a higher political office. It is not uncommon for mayors in Northern Ireland to graduate to the assembly but for some reason it is less common in the rest of the UK. Nevertheless the exposure and experience can help if you are aiming for a role like leader of the council or even a member of parliament.

 Twenty-first century mayor

Meg Hillier was a dynamic and youthful Mayor of Islington. She went on to become an MP and chair the influential Public Accounts Committee.

Staying non-political

Maybe your ambitions don't involve local government. Maybe you would be keen to be more involved with a local organisation or charity. Local groups tend to be grateful for the support given to them by civic leaders.

 Twenty-first century mayor

A month before Mimi Harker OBE ended two years as Chairman of Chiltern District Council, South Bucks Hospice asked her to become their patron. She was delighted and this prestigious appointment was down to her hard work whilst in office.

Give without expectation

It pays not to plan too carefully. You just don't know where it will take you. If you do the best job you can you will give yourself the best chance of succeeding. The best advice I have for you is to give without expectation.

What to do now

Book a holiday

- Give yourself something nice to aim at. Book a relaxing break for when you finish.

Work out how you will record your time in office

- Simple or complex make sure you have a workable system. Make sure you keep photos and notes.

Support the next generation

- Find out who will succeed you. Then help them, involve them and share your knowledge.

Do you have any aims for when you finish?

- Just do a good job and you will get to where you need to go.

Twenty-first century smile

'All my life I've felt ordinary and, right now, I'm feeling extraordinary'.

Marion Maxwell, Lord Mayor of Norwich 2016-2017

You are going to be a great civic leader. Now that you have worked through the programme you are ready to go out and excel. You have put in a huge amount of effort and for that you will be rewarded. But more than that you are equipped, you are prepared. You have achieved something few civic leaders ever manage. You are *ready*.

Think back to the very beginning of this book when you meet Carol, the archetypal underprepared mayor. She was:

- Nervous and scared

- Lacking in skills

- Short on direction

- Without support

You were a bit like that when you started this book too. Now think of the difference. Take a moment to consider how far you have come.

You have proved that you are a leader. Because you are prepared to go further than other people and because of the effort you have put in you have developed:

- The skills you need to fulfil your office

- A clear vision for your time

- A team to push you to the next level

- The support of senior councillors and staff

- A brilliant one-page civic plan

Ready to engage

Because you have all these great resources at your disposal it will be easy for you to fulfil the role of a twenty-first century mayor. That means you will deliver value to your council. You will become its human face. You will share its message far and wide. But most important of all you will connect your council with your community.

You will be a great servant and a great ambassador for you council.

But you also serve your community and you are primed to have a real impact on it. Your vision will reverberate around your neighbourhood. Your events will attract huge numbers of people. Your projects will deliver results that outlast your time in office.

You will be a great servant and a great ambassador for your community.

Go forth and inspire

Now you are ready it is time to go and do your job. So get out into your community. Meet people and be sparkling. Share your vision and bring people on board. But most of all don't busy yourself with buffets, have *an impact*.

You are going to be brilliant. You are going to be a twenty-first century mayor, you are going to be *more* than a chain.

More than an author

Duncan has always been involved in politics. He first stood in an election at twenty-two and having hung around on Abingdon Town Council for long enough they put a chain around his neck at thirty-two. People said he changed expectations of what a mayor should be. His dynamic, down to earth approach was certainly a breath of fresh air.

After he had stood down he found people kept asking him for advice. They wanted to know how they could inject the same passion and personality into their time in office. Never one to do things by half Duncan set about developing a system to help people get ready for the challenge of being a civic leader.

He realised he needed to get examples of best practice from across the country. He set about getting to know mayors and chairs through social media, local papers and word of mouth. As a result, he has worked with civic leaders from all parts of the UK and even a few from Australia and the USA. The culmination of this work is the system contained in this book.

Duncan rather sensibly married his mayoress Sreeja. They live in Abingdon with their beautiful daughter Leela. As yet she has expressed no interest in politics but then she is only two years old. In his spare time Duncan is a morris dancer. A few years ago, he was elected Mock Mayor of Ock Street meaning he is probably the only person in the world to have been a civic mayor and a mock mayor. He is also very good at making soup.

To discuss how Duncan can help you and your council you can contact him on info@theciviccoach.com.

Visit TheCivicCoach.com

You should add TheCivicCoach.com to your favourites bar. It is packed full of useful resources for civic leaders. You'll find eBooks, webinars and an extensive video library to help you become a great connection between your council and your community. And of course, you can download the workbook at www.theciviccoach.com/mtc-workbook/

But there is more to the website than that. It hosts the popular More Than a Chain blog, vlog and podcast. Every week you will find new articles about life as a civic leader. Ranging from speaking and online skills to examples of excellence in civic leadership. It is your one stop shop for tips and tricks to help you inspire your community. Visit TheCivicCoach.com to find out more.

The National Network for Civic Leaders

The National Network for Civic Leaders was founded by group of former mayors and council chairs to improve the quality of civic leadership across the nation. It helps its members by sharing best practice, celebrating excellence and offering genuine support. Its first major event was The Unchained Civic Conference in October 2017.

To catch all the action from The Unchained Civic Conference and to stay up to date with all the latest news from the network sign up here:

www.civicleaders.co.uk.

Acknowledgements

Editing
- Robin Triggs
- Richard Hagen

Cover design and layout
- Andrew Conway Hyde

Additional design
- Ismael Design
- Essetino Artists

Priceless advice
- Graham Jones
- Jan Greenough